Ceremonies from the Heart
for Children, Adults and the Earth

by

Robin White Turtle Lysne,
M.A., M.F.A., Ph.D.

⊚Blue Bone Books⊚
Santa Cruz, CA

To Ash & Neale —
may this inspire
your family
♡ Robin
Lysne

Ceremonies from the Heart
for Children, Adults and the Earth

Table Of Contents

Introduction viii

Section One ‑ Living the Sacred Every Day viii
Chapter One - Getting Started 2
Chapter Two - Creating Ceremonies from the Heart 6

Section Two – Transitions for Every Stage and Age 17
Chapter Three - Honoring Parenthood - Conception Celebration 18
Chapter Four - Birth: Preparing for Your Baby 22
Chapter Five - Birth: the Moment of Arrival   24
Chapter Six - A Naming Ceremony 26
Chapter Seven - Celebrating the First Adult Action 29
Chapter Eight - Adolescent Passages and Sexual Identity 31
Chapter Nine – Adolescent Rites for Children 43
Chapter Ten - Honoring Passages for Boys to Men 61
Chapter Eleven - Adolescent Passages for Girls - A Group Ritual,
          Mountain Art Center Adventure 67
Chapter Twelve - Honoring Who You Are as You Are 72
Chapter Thirteen - Honoring Menses 74
Chapter Fourteen - A Womanhood Celebration 78
Chapter Fifteen - Self-Discovery Ritual 87
Chapter Sixteen - Miscarriage 94
Chapter Seventeen - Abortion 98
Chapter Eighteen - Purification 103
Chapter Nineteen - Menopause 107

Section Three – Honoring Personal Transitions 111
Chapter Twenty - Starting Over - A Birthday Celebration 112
Chapter Twenty-One - Career Changes 117
Chapter Twenty-Two - A Dream Ceremony 122
Chapter Twenty-Three - Rape Recovery 127
Chapter Twenty-Four - Moving Out 132
Chapter Twenty-Five - Moving In 136
Chapter Twenty-Six - Surgery and Life-Threatening Changes 190
Chapter Twenty-Seven - Ceremony for Lost Body Parts 144

Ceremonies
from the Heart
for Children, Adults and the Earth

by

Robin White Turtle Lysne,
M.A., M.F.A., Ph.D.

Publishers Page:

Blue Bone Books
P.O. Box 2250
Santa Cruz, CA 95063-2250

ISBN: 978-1-948675-00-0
Library of Congress number: 2018910114

Editors: Mary Jane Ryan for *Dancing Up the Moon*
Robin Lysne for *Ceremonies from the Heart*

Blue Bone Books is a cooperative poetry press also
publishing children's, spiritual books.

Section Four - Honoring Relationships 147
Chapter Twenty-Eight - A New Relationship 148
Chapter Twenty-Nine - Friendship Changes 151
Chapter Thirty - A Unique Wedding 155
Chapter Thirty-One - Honoring the Mother of the Bride 158
Chapter Thirty-Two - Acknowledging Divorce 161
Chapter Thirty-Three - Two Funerals 166
Chapter Thirty-Four - Respecting Living Elders 172

Section Five - Rites with the Natural World 177
Chapter Thirty-Five - Natural Disasters 178
Chapter Thirty-Six - Rites with the Earth 184
Chapter Thirty-Seven – Fire Circles 193
Conclusion 196
About the Author 197
Acknowledgements 198
Resources 203
Sources 204
Endnotes 207

Dedication

To the families of the modern world,
may they use these transitional ceremonies
to support their families unto the seventh generation,
no matter what religion or spiritual tradition.

Ceremonies from the Heart

for Children, Adults and the Earth

Introduction

"When you are in accord with nature, nature will yield up it's bounty...and every sacred place is the place where eternity shines through time."

Joseph Campbell, Mythos III, The Shaping
of the Western Tradition

Ceremonies from the Heart offers ways, for those who wish to be empowered, to create community and mark life transitions in families. It also helps us to learn directly from the Earth what she needs to heal from humanities destructive tendencies.

In its original form this book was called *Dancing Up the Moon, A Woman's Guide to Creating Traditions that Bring Sacredness to Daily Life*, published by Conari Press, Berkeley in 1995. It was developed from my thesis on rites of passage for teens from The Institute in Culture and Creation Spirituality housed at Holy Names College, Oakland, CA, and was inspired by a rite of initiation in my own family that I helped to initiate and create prior to attending school. That rite, the Blue Heron Ceremony, is one you can read about in this book.

Since *Dancing Up the Moon* went out of print in 1999, I have dreamed of an expanded version of the book including rites for men as well as women, as well as people of mixed or various genders. I wanted to create rites for communities that could help them initiate their children in a secular society and support youth development in a positive way. Lastly, I wanted ways for people to commune with the Earth in a sacred manner that could change our view of the Earth from commodity to sacred ground.

Ceremonies from the Heart goes beyond *Dancing Up the Moon* in several ways. In addition to offering rites for women and men and differently gendered people, it also includes community rites based on the seasons, phases of the moon and land configurations. This is important to help us celebrate the cycles of the seasons and to honor the Earth as sacred.

The Earth does not need us to survive, but we need her without a doubt in order to live. She is alive, a living being, who feeds and supports us in every way. The Earth and her creatures are essential to our well being, not something to fight off, make into a commodity, destroy, or manage to death. Without such a fundamental relationship shift with the Earth, humans are in danger of destroying the very life we say we cherish, because not one of us can live here without our Mother Earth. She is the

Divine Mother as embodied in the Earth. We must fall in love with nature again with a sense of awe, as our ancestors did every day in the fields, near the sea or in the wild forest. When we love the miracle of life we are immersed in daily, we are less likely to destroy what we love. Heart-felt ceremonies can help, even for those locked in cities where nature seems quite remote or unacknowledged.

One question that has formed this book is: What do rites of passage actually do? When you look at them from the outside, they are as various as the cultures that created them. However, on the inside people use combinations of fasting, food, clothing and ceremony to initiate members of the community into life's amazing stages and cycles. Their appearance may be very different, but the function is the same cross-culturally. That is to support and mark significant movement from one phase of life to another. The outer is to support inner deeper changes within the self. They create our stories, mark turning points, and therefore create the mythology we are living now.

Rites of passage have been celebrated cross-culturally since people first sat around campfires together and acknowledged connections. Marriages, births, manhood, womanhood, death, and birthdays have been celebrated with feasts, toasts, and forms of physical identification such as rings, scarring, circumcision, tattooing, dress, ritual baths and hairstyle changes for as long as people have been living in cultural groups. They are a way to bring people together, to connect in celebration important transitions and to underscore life passages.

Ceremonies or rituals are time-tested ways to reconnect with our selves, our friends, and families with nature. This book is intended to encourage and support your transitions that in turn will bring you a more meaning-filled life. As you do, you will be engaging more harmony with the Earth as well as with your self in your personal evolution. It can serve to reconnect disenfranchised children, especially boys, who need to be more connected with their communities.

This book is intended to lay a new groundwork and framework for all of us who are looking for rites that will support us through the next millennia whether we are in a religious tradition or not. It does not create a new dogma, but empowers people to come into their power to find their own stories valuable within their families. This creates greater meaning. This greater meaning can be the new cosmic story of our time, or our new mythology. We are all forming that new story together. *Ceremonies from the Heart* can be instrumental in that change.

Religious groups have initiations that help to bring citizens into churches, temples and parishes through organized religion. All these rites serve an important purpose. However, as people move away from organized religions in contemporary society and become more integrated racially and ethnically, the rites once held by organized religions are becoming less meaningful to contemporary culture.1

In Judeo-Christian religions we must learn to embrace nature as part of ourselves, and therefore throw off the old destructive ideas of the struggle of man against or over nature. Humanity must learn a new level of working *with* nature as companion. Joseph Campbell, who I would call the Godfather of Myth in the 21st century and author of many books on mythology, ritual and culture, said in a lecture late in his life:

"Mythology, when it is operating socially, serves four functions. The first, the mystical function, opens up a realization of the mystical dimension: that behind the surface phenomenology of the world there is a transcendent mystery source, and that source is also within ourselves.

"The second function, the cosmological function, has to do with our image of the world. This changes radically from time to time. In the early hunting-and-gathering societies, with relatively small horizons, science reflected the visible: the sun rose, it went down; the moon rose, it went down. Copernicus changed all this: "The sun isn't rising; it's we who are turning." The cosmology totally changed along with the science. A mythology, to be up-to-date and really to work in the minds of people living in the modern scientific world, must itself incorporate the modern scientific world.

"The third function of a mythology is sociological: to validate and maintain a certain specific social order, here and now, of a specific society.

"The fourth function is the pedagogical, guiding the individual harmoniously through the inevitable crises of the stages of life in his world in terms of its goods, its values, and its dangers. There is no conflict between mysticism and science, but there is a conflict between science of the 2000 BC and that of 2000 AD. We have gotten stuck with an image of the Universe that is about as childish as we can imagine. We need poets and seers that will give us a transcendent vision of the Universe in the world in which we are living now."

What is the mythology of our time that can give us a connection to the universe, as well as our personal universe? Certainly the first moon walk gave us a unified vision on one Earth, a bright blue marble floating in space. Some movies such as Star Wars, and Harry Potter, give us visions of other worlds, and personal power through heroic acts.

But in the real world how are people without a religious foundation, who consider themselves spiritual, going to celebrate the passages that are part of life and create that new transcendent vision for our future? We need a guidebook. *Ceremonies from the Heart* is that guidebook.

As we move faster and faster with technology and our cities grow to engulf smaller communities in an ever widening band of the urban landscape, we often have forgotten about the importance of celebrating times of transition without cell phones, I-pods or computers. We have also moved away from nature, which is one way traditional indigenous cultures have always celebrated rites of passage, in part to help citizens integrate with nature in a more intimate and loving relationship. Honoring the sacred nature of Earth fundamentally changes our relationship with her.

This book is an attempt to give us the tools to create our own rites of passage no matter for what occasion, and to help us bring our culture closer to nature and our personal stories within the greater universe.

Earth-based rites give every human the tools they need to live here in harmony. This is an interdenominational book not based on any tradition, except the Earth that is; the four directions, the four winds, the four seasons, etc. It can be used by anyone, inside a religious framework or outside one in any part of the world. It all starts with changing our fundamental relationship with ourselves as Universes within the greater Universe.

This is the mythology of today based on science and backed up by what we discover scientifically everyday. When recognize our personal universe within the greater Universe, we feel empowered to create and sustain ourselves, and future generations by creating meaningful passages for our families and our communities. It helps us deepen our sense of place within sacred time and space.

We, as ordinary citizens, can create rites and rituals that matter and empower. Many people want and need deeper meaning in their lives. Creating more meaningful ceremonies bring that about. Meaningful rituals help us take responsibility for our spiritual lives as well as our physical and emotional ones. The truth is, whether we surrender our spiritual relationship with the divine to an institution or not, we are ultimately responsible for our spiritual relationship with All-That-Is in any case.

Since there has been so much trust broken by patriarchal institutions both religious and secular, it is time to reconsider our spiritual and cultural connections with those institutions that have broken trust with us. In doing so we can create our own communities and circles, and many people already have.

One way to reconsider our relationship with these institutions is to take our spiritual power back from them. As people take their spiritual power back from some of the institutions that have traditionally held these ceremonies in trust with the people, individuals can learn to offer rites if they know how. This book is intended to show them how. These institutions can still support community, however, as we each take responsibility for our personal relationship with the divine, we only enrich ourselves through more depth of meaning and experience with an honoring ceremony. We need new and more personal ways to initiate ourselves into various phases of life. In doing so we empower ourselves in our communities to bring people together and create more meaningful lives. The truth is that we are ultimately responsible for our relationship with the Divine, institution or no institution.

My hope is that these stories of rites that I share with you, will offer new ways to support an emerging culture. That new culture is calling us to be all we can be in every facet of our lives. In addition to personal rites that we can share and create, this book will help you develop a new relationship with the Earth. As we respect what we receive from her everyday, we will stop exploiting her bounty.

Thankfully thousands of people are beginning to realize they can make a difference by changing the course of our self-destructive human behavior. This book is a guide for how we can develop a new relationship with life affirming relationship with the Earth—individually, culturally and spiritually—inside a church or outside one with a new cosmic order springing from within. We have to come back to nature and see the Divine Mother as the sustainer of our lives on this planet. We live in a cosmos that is alive! All of it is reflected in our inner universal self and within our communities.

> Myth, is the secret opening through which the inexhaustible
> energies of the cosmos pour into human cultural manifestation…
>
> Joseph Campbell[2]

From the inside, rites can be life changing events that help us transition into the new part of our lives and engage in age-old stories that our cultures cherish. Rites bring us into the moment and help us face what is in our world today. They help us become more accepting and connected to each other and nature, while at the same time, support individuation and community responsibility to unite us to our current cultural mythos.

In some cases rites help us become more divine and acknowledge and aligned us with whatever forces of the Universe created us in the first place.

This life force that lives through us, is unconditional love. Think about it, the life force that lives all things, accepts everything as it is. In my books, *Heart Path*, and *Heart Path Handbook*,3 I teach self-love and ways to align with our life force and accept ourselves as we are. Inside the self, as one loves oneself more, internal changes take place in our personal growth and we move from fear and anger to love. When we love ourselves, we love others more. Ultimately we may have a teacher that shows us how to transcend the ego and surrender to our authentic selves. (Jesus, Buddha, Yogananda, Guru Mai, Amma, Adiyashanti, Ananda Moia Ma, there are many more). This work takes place in these books mentioned above. So if you want to go deeper into the self my books mentioned above can help.

Today we are at a turning point that requires us to rethink and readdress our relationship with the Earth and technology. We need to find a way to make amends with the Earth as our Mother and sustainer. We are in a time of deep cultural shifts with a need to move sustainably into the future or humanity may not make it. We are required to revisit how we relate to each other and ourselves. In other words this is an age of deep personal and global transformation that will hopefully work towards a more balanced and sane use of the Earth and establish a better relationship with her. It is my deepest concern that unless we do, we are not going to survive. This transition we are all in—calls us to embrace the Earth and ourselves as sacred—and embody our God-Nature of unconditional love in the process.

Ceremonies from the Heart helps us come together with our communities and develop our own mythos. They help us create community. While the methods and religious practices vary, the same basic elements of nature are used worldwide to do the initiating such as earth, air, fire and water. In our secular society, the same elements can be used to honor, bless and bury loved ones. Rites give voice to memories and dreams. They acknowledge, who we are and celebrate transitions for our everyday lives. They help us let go, and help us move beyond our old patterns of being to embrace our lives as we are and as we are becoming.

This is why I feel this book is so important for today's contemporary society, especially as we merge our nationalities, our economies and our cultures. If those institutions that have helped us celebrate life in the past no longer work for us, we still need ways to move through life with celebrations that matter to us and bring more meaning everyday.

It is my hope that these rites are seeds of ideas for your own life and for generations to come. They might help our culture as a whole begin to live in a truly sustainable relationship with the Earth and with our fellow humans.

Use it as a touchstone reference book for celebrations of all kinds. We can find ways to deepen meaning with each other and within ourselves. We need the Earth, and she needs us to wake up. Let's take hold together and celebrate the amazing gifts we are given every day by the Earth, and the Universe, celebrating life as one family.

For all my relations,

Robin White Turtle Lysne

SECTION ONE

LIVING THE SACRED EVERY DAY

1
Getting Started

Marking passage and cycles of the seasons are ways that we can honor the sacred in our every day lives. As we organize parties, send cards, and cook the food for birthdays, holidays, weddings, and graduations, we are honoring the existence and importance of others in our lives. What are we actually doing by these actions? We make connections, acknowledge loved ones, bond our families, and mark life passages. We celebrate the lives of others. Intuitively we create a mood or atmosphere for each event.

In this book you will find ways that extend naturally from what we already do. In addition, you will find ways we can create new rites to help us become a closer relative to the Earth.

Through true stories of my passages and those of others, *Ceremonies from the Heart* shows you how to mark important turning points in your life. By sharing experiences of living in a sacred way, I hope to point to ways that bring more meaning to our lives. It is my greatest joy to share with you ways to honor the sacred. The process has helped to love myself, and others more, and bring loved ones closer together. It has shifted the emphasis in my life from a material-based existence emphasized by the culture at large, where my self-esteem and measure of success were based largely on income, to a spiritual one, where I know I am sacred, and the world around me is too, and I live out of that moment to moment experience.

Our lives are full of important changes. Birth, marriage, and death are most commonly celebrated, as they are the transitions that traditionally have the most impact on our lives. By celebrating only these events, however, it becomes all to easy to speed our way through the rest of life without much thought to what happens in between.

The first section, Living the Sacred Everyday, lays the groundwork to living a more sacred life every day with regards to the Earth. It shares how to create a ritual. Section Two –Rite for Every Stage at Every Age, offers ways to create ceremonies that reconnect us through various rites of passage for different stages of our lives from birth to menopause. It speaks to ways we can make our daily lives more sacred through personal rites of passage. In the third section, Rites for Personal Transitions offers ways to help us in transitions where I have included transitions of family and career, moving in or out, dreams surgery, and more; section Four- Honoring Relationships gives respect to wedding, divorce and death; and section Five Rites with the Natural World, offers some ideas to connect with nature and help us pass on rites we can develop with the Earth to help her and our own transformations.

You will notice that I focused primarily on transitions not celebrated in the culture at large. They are, namely, childhood transitions; rites of passage for girls and boys, and for women menses and menopause, pregnancy, birth, miscarriage, abortion, and rape recovery; rites of purification, changing or starting careers; changing residences; relationship rites; and the transitions of divorce and illness, new rites of death, and rites with the Earth.

Use it as a reference book to inspire you. As you read it through, you may begin to see a new worldview opening up before you that may inspire you to new relationships with yourself, others and the Earth through acknowledging your own story. Each of us has our own inner wisdom and unique path to follow. You know what is right and most significant for you. My intention is to empower you to find your own way, not to create a new dogma or sell a new theology.

Marking transitions in life is creating a rite of passage, a phrase coined by anthropologist Arnold Van Gennep in his 1909 book *The Rites of Passage*. The word rite, or ritual, comes from the Latin ritus, or river. Life-force, or spirit, is like a river that flows through every living thing. When we take time to mark a passage, we are dipping into the river of life, or making a ritual. Matthew Fox states in his book *Reinventing Work,* "only ritual teaches us to honor the sacred." We bless our bodies, minds, and souls. We celebrate, we grieve, and share our journey with those we love. Chapters Eight through Eleven will go into more detail of the psychological importance for adolescence.

Because our daily activities become the context for remembering our connection to everything around us; washing dishes, cleaning, diapering, driving, working, and communicating, I use poetry to express how we bring our spirit, our presence, into the physical world at the beginning of each chapter. Poetry re-creates and marks moments in time. I hope it inspires you to find your unique method of celebrating the everyday as sacred.

Whether we acknowledge the sacred daily or create once-in-a-lifetime rites of passage, the key to living a richer, more sacred life is moving from our hearts. Our hearts are the center of life force in our physical bodies. The love in our spiritual hearts radiates from our souls and connects us to life.

When we create a meaningful sacred event, assisting ourselves through a transitional phase, it is a self-loving act. We re-connect ourselves to our personal cosmology. We companion ourselves. We listen to our hearts and act on what is called for. Isolation disappears as we share our personal stories, we have a purpose, we make a difference, we feel loved, we become love and become more a part of the world. Integration in the present moment occurs.

Rites of passage bring more awareness to our lives, simply by taking the time to do them. We need only to slow down and listen. So often when I have shared with people about the rites of passage for my nieces and nephews, or how a family celebrated the arrival of their newborn, people comment that they thought of doing something similar but hadn't acted on it.

By acting on such a fleeting thought as "I want to honor my daughter's womanhood," we shift relationship dynamics: everyone is informed of her change, denial of her growth and maturity disappears, our family and friends take on different roles in the family group. Emotions are released as we realize the child is no longer a child. Too often we let the next thought stop us: "but I don't know how . . . and I don't have time." It takes courage to create something that we have never tried before. We learn as we try. A rite can easily set new boundaries and connections at the same time. Your daughter or son is honored for and educated about their budding maturity; they are given new responsibility through the process of creating the rite. Everyone moves into more harmony with the flow of life's changes.

All of the rites are intuitively developed. Some passages are combined stories from different people's experiences. Although I have explored several cultural and religious traditions and they have influenced me, none of the rites are borrowed from other cultures unless specified. In those cases, I share the source and express deep gratitude for those traditions.

While these rituals seem personal to me, I have discovered that by listening to my needs and what I know is true about myself, I have created support for myself and built my self-esteem. What I have discovered is that when I "fill my own cup first," validating and nurturing who I am, I can then give from "the overflow" with more health and vitality. I have more support to offer others. This is contrary to what our culture traditionally teaches, especially women. But our example of self-nurturing and care can validate and encourage others to do the same.

All of us have a lot in common as different hues of the same human family. We are all in bodies; we eat, sleep, work, and carry on bodily functions in similar ways. We all have a mother and father who have shaped us, whether they are with us physically or not. We need food, clothing, and shelter to survive. We are dependent on nature and are a part of nature. We need love, acknowledgment, and beauty to feed our souls. As unique drops of the great flowing river, we each require love, respect, and safety to be vulnerable and share from our hearts during transitions.

We also have differences, which make us unique. No matter what your ethnic, cultural, or religious background, your personal experiences are important. Your career, marital status, or sexual orientation, your choices, creative ventures, likes and dislikes can endow your rituals with deep personal meaning. Our actions create a legacy for ourselves and loved ones whether we are conscious of it or not. We tell our personal story as we live it. Our actions matter and resonate out to the world.

By sharing my story and those of others, I hope you feel supported in yours. If I can create meaningful rites, so can you. As you turn the pages of this book, let the experiences wash over and inspire you. Then listen to your heart. You will know what to do next.

2
Creating Ceremonies from the Heart

Besides the essentials of love, respect, and safety, and the knowledge that we are part of a greater whole, there are a few things that might assist you in composing rites for yourself and your family. They have come from my personal observations while creating ceremonies over the past thirty years and from the spiritual teachers I have studied with along the way. None of the information I am sharing with you is meant to harm or invade anyone's energy field without their knowledge or permission. The first rule for successful ceremonies from the heart is to first do no harm, and the second is always to ask permission for participation from those involved. Permission coincides with universal law of free will choice, which each of us have as part of our birthright. We need to listen to what is right for us, for our highest and wisest good.

What is Sacred?

According to Webster's dictionary the term sacred has several definitions including: Consecrated to or by God; holy; having to do with religion; venerated; hallowed; inviolate. When you look up inviolate it means; not violated; kept sacred or unbroken.4 I like the last definition the best. The term 'inviolate' or 'unbroken' really relates especially to Nature as it pertains to our relationship with the elements of the Earth. When we create a rite of any kind we are creating a link, an unbroken chain of experiences, that create meaning for us. When we create a rite for and with the Earth, we are helping ourselves to come in right relationship with her. We honor ourselves and the Earth as part of this amazing web of life.

Intention

The single most important element in any rite is setting your intention. Rituals are neutral containers of the present moment. You determine by your attitude, frame of mind, and actions the positive or negative quality of that vessel as well as the flow of energy through it.

If you intend to honor yourself and others and support the changes in your life, your rite will be a positive experience. If you come with a negative frame of mind, resisting change, using the rite to control the outcome, the universe will give you a negative experience. Clarity of intention and awareness of your actions in the rite are the most important elements. It is why a period of purification and preparation occurs before many traditional rites to focus intention.

Simplicity

Keep it simple. If you find yourself creating a Broadway version of the Pope's visit to the United States, you may be missing the point. Return to what the ritual is about and use only the essentials. Complicated rites only distract you from the core meaning you are trying to convey. On the other hand, putting thought and prayer into it, with the right symbols for your life, can create much deeper meaning.

Take Your Time

Because you want to stay aware of what you are doing in the rite, it is important to take your time. I like to imagine that I am entering a "no time" dimension when I do a ritual. In this space there is nothing more important than what is happening right now. I unplug the phone, don't answer the door, make sure there is nothing else planned, and ask other participants to do the same. Most people instinctively know to do this. But occasionally there are those so hooked into their schedules, cell phones and computers they need extra permission to relax.

Know You Are Not Alone: Managing Fear

As I mentioned in the Chapter One, it takes courage to create your first ritual, especially if you have never done it before. It is always scary to change and begin something new. That is part of the creative process. This book is designed to be a friend on the path. Others have gone before you. Their stories are here to guide you. It is normal to be afraid; and it is part of our evolution to go for it anyway, knowing we are supporting growth and greater expression of love.

Many times I have been afraid of looking silly or stupid. Sometimes I was afraid of not being able to speak the truth. What I have discovered is that people respond to being sincere. They can feel your intention, as well as hear it. If you are coming from the heart, that is all you need.

Part of the fear of a ritual is facing the unknown. We don't always know how the universe will create our new experiences. At some point, if we set our intention, come from our hearts, and do the ritual sincerely, the universe responds in kind.

Often the biggest challenge is letting go and trusting the process, which means dropping the need to control beyond what we are truly responsible for, and leaving enough room for spontaneity. It is intuition and spontaneity that make each rite unique, even if the format is the same every time.

Nature As Teacher

Every ritual throughout history has been based on nature. The four elements—earth, air, fire, and water— have been used to invoke blessing and remembrance and recount scripture or sacred stories. In Eastern cultures there are five elements, the fifth being metal. In most Native American traditions of this hemisphere there are four and metal is incorporated into earth.

Every art form, science, technology, and method of work are based on nature as well. Think about it! We cannot live apart from the earth. Nature provides us everything we need to survive and thrive. Nature is infinitely ancient, various, and creative and constantly changing.

No matter where we live on the globe, there are four elements and seven directions: north, east, south, west, the earth, sky, and the center, all of which describe our place in the vast context of the natural world. Our bodies contain all four elements of the earth. Each element relates to aspects of human nature and can symbolize for us a myriad of things.

Various indigenous cultures use different colors to symbolize the four directions. The differences depend on where they live, the terrain, the wind and weather patterns, seasonal fluctuations, and traditions they have learned from their families (see "Be Aware of How You Pass It Around" later in this chapter.)

The following information has come from the book *The Sacred Pipe* by Lakota Sioux Elder Black Elk, the reading I have done the oral teachings I have attended in various circles, and my personal experience. It's provided here for those of you unfamiliar with the symbols of the four directions and what they represent. You may want to investigate colors and directions that are used by indigenous people in your area, or develop your own awareness by spending time in nature and getting in touch with the land you live on. Various South American cultures also use the same directions, they just use the elements in a different order. But in fact, all indigenous cultures use these elements as the basis for their rituals. All religions use the elements too. (Water for blessing, earth for the altar, fire for the candles, air for songs.)5

When I was studying in Brazil, I learned about the Orixá's that is another name for the sacred energies of the four elements. The name stems from Africa originally. The most surprising thing was that I learned and felt was that each of us are an element or combinations of elements that make your particular Orixá. Since then, it has helped me relate to people who ask "what do you see" when they come to me for information or advice. As you read through the following, think about what elements you most relate to, and which ones you don't as easily. These can inform you of your Orixa, though in most cases, your Orixa has to be determined through some kind of ritual in a tradition that supports Orixa wisdom.

The Seven Directions Symbolic Meaning

South

Relations, roots, grounding, earth, healing, home, stability, soil, inheritance, the color red, metal, stones, established, contained, the cycle of
birth and death. A bowl of earth or a red cloth can be used to honor this direction in your rite.

North

Mind, intelligence, power, the ethereal, life-force, invisible presence, air, spirit, the color white, cold, where storms come from in winter. An empty bowl or white cloth can be used to symbolize this direction.

East

Transformation, letting go, new beginnings, masculine principle, logic, what can be seen, rising sun, heat, fire, the color yellow. A candle or yellow cloth can symbolize this direction.

West

Feminine principle, emotions, flexibility, water, fluidity, nourishment, the unknown, the color black. A bowl of water or a black cloth can symbolize this direction.

Earth

In addition, the earth is symbolized by the color green. It is said that Grandmother Earth heals all things. Indeed, all vitamins, minerals, and medications come originally from the earth. Water is the lifeblood of the earth. The earth is considered feminine by most indigenous cultures. Earth is the fifth direction.

Sky

The sky is symbolized by the color blue. Grandfather Sky is the sustainer of life. The air we breathe, the stars we travel by, the weather, which brings rain, all comes from the sky. Sky is considered masculine and is the sixth direction.

Center

The center is where all the directions converge, the center of the wheel of life, and of our being. It is the heart, unconditional love, the I AM, self-realization. It is the seventh direction.

In most Earth-based traditions, the Creator is neutral and loves all creations equally, no matter where you are on the wheel, whether you are animal or mineral.

Each element contains positive and negative aspects. It is said that as we move through life, we move in a clockwise direction, facing the center around the medicine wheel, from one direction to the other. When we are in the north, or in our power, we face south, the direction of home, surrender, family, birth, and death. When we are in the east, the direction of new beginnings, we face west, the direction of the unknown. We are reminded constantly of the apparent opposite of where we are, humbling us to the realities of life.

When we are in transition, we are moving from one direction to the other. Rituals can reflect these changes by using one or more of the colors symbolizing the direction. For example, if you feel you are moving from the west, or the unknown, represented by the color black, into your power, or north, symbolized by the color white, you can use colored cloths in the ritual. You can either wear these colors or use them on the altar; this gives you an opportunity to acknowledge your movement around the wheel.

Sometimes we move toward the center of the wheel, where we can see everything spinning around us. Our spinal alignment becomes very important, because the medicine wheel, or wheel of life is reflected in the body. If you place the wheel at the top of the head, the front of us is water, or emotions, the back, will or east, the sides are north and south, air and earth respectively. This is a time when we feel powerful, present, soft and strong simultaneously. Balance becomes the most critical focus when you are in the center. You feel into your core, and move from there, always in balance. We choose to walk in balance in our lives to keep our equilibrium and to stay present. The Native Americans use a circle with the equidistant cross in the center to symbolize the four directions, earth, sky, and the center.

The best description I have read of nature as teacher is found in the late Angeles Arrien's book, *The Four Fold Way: Walking the Path of the Warrior, Teacher, Healer, and Visionary*. She has researched many nature-based shamanic traditions throughout the world and describes four principles that are found in virtually all of them. These are very helpful to keep in mind when creating a ritual.

* Show up, or choose to be present. Being present allows us to access the human resources of power, presence, and communication. This is the way of the warrior.

* Pay attention to what has heart and meaning. Paying attention opens us to the human resources of love, gratitude, acknowledgment, and validation. This is the way of the healer.

* Tell the truth without blame or judgment. Nonjudgmental truthfulness maintains our authenticity and develops our inner vision and intuition. This is the way of the visionary.

* Be open to outcome, not attached to outcome. Openness and nonattachment help us recover the human resources of wisdom and objectivity. This is the way of the teacher.

The principles are expressed through the four archetypes: the warrior, the healer, the visionary, and the teacher. They are four aspects of our inner nature in balance and harmony with the universe.

I find these four principles extraordinary and use them daily to check my approach to life. They are my touchstones to authenticity. I also use them in creating rituals.

Universal Symbols

There are also shapes used by people around the world that can affect the psychology of the rite as well as convey a deeper meaning. Whether people sit or stand in a circle, in rows, or in a square, the shape can affect one's sense of place and helps to shape the feeling of the rite. A configuration of straight rows of people facing a speaker, for example, lends itself to more authoritarian presentations; it also accommodates large groups of people. However, it is most natural for people to congregate in a circle in family-sized groups. For centuries we have gathered around campfires and sat in circles for stories and discussions. The circle represents wholeness, according to Angeles Arrien in her book, *Signs of Life: The Five Universal Shapes and How to Use Them*. In my own experience of being in circle gatherings, I feel both a part of the group yet an individual at the same time.

Through my work with clients and in my spiritual practice, I have realized that all symbols are based on nature, many on the human body. Here is an overview of shapes and how I have come to interpret them, through my work and with the help of Arrien's book:

Circle: wholeness, completion, continuation, inclusion.

Triangle: symbol of womanhood, the Delta of Venus; mother,

maiden, crone; or mother, father, child.

Vertical line or bar: masculine principle, fertility, examples; the maypole, sword, or straight weapon.

Square: the mind, order, structure, framework, agreement, stability.

Spiral: growth, continuation, regeneration, change.

Oval: a sign of spirit. Oval portraits of religious figures were often used throughout art history to represent the most divine beings.

Cross: the extended arms of a human, head at one end and legs together forming the other extension. They meet at the level of the heart, the center of all things. As you may well know, the crucifix is an old Christian symbol, but its existence predates Christianity, and it is found throughout the world.

Equidistant cross: relationship, integration, and balanced connection. The equidistant cross is the center of the medicine wheel, and symbolizes the four directions, the four seasons, the four winds, and the four corners of the universe. I consider it the symbol for our time, as we need it now more than ever.

Star of David: two intersecting triangles coming together in the center forming a hexagram. The name David means beloved, so the Star of David is the symbol of the beloved. Two intersecting triangles from earth and the heavens meet in the heart center.

Five-pointed star: the shape is a human being with arms and legs extended. Its shape can also symbolize our origins from the stars. (The Lakota people believe that we came from the Milky Way and make star quilts for their babies when they are born, at other times of transition and at death.)

The medicine wheel: The symbol Native Americans use to express the four directions, as well as earth, sky, and center; their wheel of life is called the medicine wheel; a circle with and equidistant cross in the center of it. In actuality is symbolic of the Earth itself and if seen like a gyroscope, then the Earth becomes an orb.

Personal Symbols

Symbols in a ritual can bring great personal significance to whatever you are doing. From your grandmother's wedding ring to your father's Masonic pin, whatever symbols you choose, can connect your historic roots and spiritual traditions with the present. They can establish an energy pattern during a rite, and help you set your intention more firmly. I urge you to discover what has meaning for you and do not be afraid to use it for fear of seeming silly or too personal. What matters is what has meaning.

Using Symbols in Your Rite

If you feel an affinity to them, symbols can bring greater meaning to your rite; they can deepen the meaning of a ritual and help us better understand the forces of nature and the processes of life and death. If you choose not to use them, however, they are not necessary. The form you use is not as important as the clarity of your intention.

Whether or not you choose to use them, you may find yourself unable to avoid symbols! How you sit together, the patterns of dancing, the procession into or out of a space, the shape of the altar, or the elements used on it-all play a part in the rite. Pay attention to what attracts and feels natural to you, and the unfolding ceremony will teach you which symbols are personally important.

An Altar

It is not necessary to have an altar; however, one can be used to create a central theme, encourage group participation, or honor several traditions at once. An altar is simple to construct. You can place a scarf in the center of the floor, or take a box, small table, or chair and cover it with the colors of the four directions, for example. You can then place something meaningful to you in the center: a ring, a photo, a book, or whatever works for you. A white cloth is a good universal color that combines all of the colors in the light spectrum, as black combines all colors of Earth.

Be Aware of How You Pass It Around

The direction that you pass things in the ritual can also contribute to its meaning. Johnny Moses, a Native American teacher and keeper of his tradition on the Northwest Coast, says that prevailing winds can determine the direction to pass bowls, candles, cedar smoke (or smudge), or other artifacts in a ritual. On his island the prevailing winds move counterclockwise, so that is the direction they pass objects. In other cultures, for example on the Great Plains, it is traditional to pass things from right to left, or clockwise, which is the direction of the prevailing winds.

In most earth-based traditions, the clockwise passing of ritual objects is affirmative, and counterclockwise passing supports dismantling or letting go. If you were releasing a part of your life--say a job, or emotions over a loss--passing things counterclockwise would represent letting go. However, you may want to move things clockwise as a general rule, to affirm change, a new job, or other positive aspects of your life.

It can matter which way you decide pass objects, and it may depend entirely on the nature of the rite, the prevailing winds in your area, or simply what feels right at the time. Passing clockwise is generally gathering or affirming, and passing counter-clockwise is letting go and ending. What matters most is that your intention is clear and positive.

Your personal belief systems will also determine what you decide to do. I suggest you choose what feels right to you and stick to it as your primary direction and don't switch off, unless you deliberately shift for a specific purpose. Consistency helps set your overall intention more firmly, and you won't have to reestablish your groundwork every time.

Telling Your Story

Our life stories are the experiences that form us, help us grow, and give meaning to our lives. They are important, as our personal mythology. A rite becomes a segment of your personal story. It can gather parts of your past together in conclusion to move to the next step into the future. A rite should have a beginning, middle, and end, just like your life.

In The Rites of Passage, Arnold Van Gennep observed and defined the beginning of a rite as separation, the middle as transition, and the end as incorporation. Chapter Eight goes into more detail.

During a ritual, various segments can be emphasized, depending on the nature of the rite. For example, in an adolescent rite separation may take up the initial phase, and transition and incorporation, the majority of the ritual. A funeral may emphasize separation and transition through mourning and the funeral itself, whereas incorporation may be dealt with at the end of the funeral in the form of prayers or offerings for the soul of the deceased, and may extend into the grieving process.

As I reflected on the rituals I have created, I could identify the stages Van Gennep delineated. His observations give form to the intuitive process.

Parties, Celebrations, Rituals, and Ceremonies

For clarity, here are some definitions. Parties and celebrations are basically the same thing: a gathering of people having a good time. Celebrations can be for an entire city, whereas parties are generally smaller. Rituals can be a segment of the party, or the whole event if it is thought of in the context of marking a transition. A ceremony is a ritual, although not necessarily spiritual in nature, for example, an awards ceremony, graduation, or honors ceremony. In this book you can make the assumption that I am always speaking of a spiritual context, therefore I use ceremony and ritual interchangeably.

A ritual draws this distinction: it is a point in time when we consciously make a transition from one way of life to another. It can be fun or not; it holds all possibilities. It is not necessarily a party or a celebration, but it can be, just as parties and celebrations can be rituals if the intention is stated as such and the actions are carried out to correspond with the intention.

Rituals can be fun as well as meaningful. Spontaneity and humor can be as much a part of a rite as anything. Some of my favorite rites are centered around a meal where humor is part of the fabric of the celebration. So long as you don't loose focus for long, humor can bond and heal people. A great deal depends on the attitude of those leading the event and how they set the tone for other participants.

How to Use This Book

To begin creating your own rituals, I suggest you read the appropriate story and think of the following questions:

* What do you intend for your rite, or what is the single most important thing you want to do by holding this ceremony?

* What new way of being are you embracing?

* What are you letting go of in order to welcome the change?

* Whom would you like to be there?

* What location suits you?

* What symbols, if any, do you want to include?

* What is your story and how does that play into the rite?

* What do you want to do for the beginning, middle, and end of your rite?

* Do you have a favorite poem or story that enhances your intention?

* Unless it is a mourning rite or one for letting go of a negative experience, enjoy yourself! Rites can be fun and humorous.

Anything can become an expression of the sacred or the inviolate. If we want to live life in a sacred manner, we simply need to be present to life and bring love to everything we do. Then we are automatically developing a relationship to All-That-Is, all the time.

We become love as we love more and as we practice being what we are authentically; sacred beings embedded in a continuous flow of life.

The following are stories of rites created by myself and other people. At the end of each chapter there are questions to inspire your ritual.

SECTION TWO

RITES FOR EVERY STAGE AND AGE

3
Honoring Parenthood

Conception

Beginning
Now Is The Time . . .
Come to me, come to me,
now the two of us shall be three,
two, by grace, shall be three.

Terry and Christine wanted to conceive a child. They had planned to start a family after they were both settled into their careers.

Christine knew of a simple ritual they could do that would affirm their spiritual connection and welcome the baby. Before bed one night, Christine lit a candle to honor the union between them.

She said, "Terry, I am so glad you're my mate; you are going to be a great father." She passed the candle to him. He looked at the candle and paused.

Then he blew out the flame. "What are you doing, Terry!" Christine said, startled.

Terry jumped off of the bed and shouted at her, "I can't do this. I feel like this is your idea, and you have just handed me a script. Now I'm suppose to say this stuff to you. Well, I don't like the way you are setting this up. I don't like the way you are talking to me, and I feel like a playmate who is suppose to follow your rules."

"Christine, I want a child with you, but I need to be included in this, if that's what were doing—a ritual. We should do this together. I want to be included in the process."

Christine was shocked and upset. She sat and glared at Terry while he made his case. Then she heard the last thing he said to her: "I want to be included . . ." She looked at him painfully and replied, "You're right. I'm sorry, Honey. I didn't mean to take over. What do you want to do?"

Terry sank onto the end of the bed, taking a few deep breaths and absorbing Christine's apology. "I don't know," he said finally. After a long pause he continued slowly. "This may sound silly, but I want to say something to the child we are bringing into this world. I want to talk to him or her, and let the child know how much he or she is wanted. I want to tell the baby what great parents we will be, and what a great mom he'll have. I want to tell him how much fun and support and care we will give."

Then Christine looked at him shyly and said, "Do you want to light a candle? Or do you want to use something else, maybe water, for blessing each other, or burn a little sage in a shell for cleansing the air, or—"

"Wait a minute!" Terry jumped up and ran into the garage. He returned with his guitar, which he hadn't played for a while. "There's a song I used to know that I want to sing."

This wasn't what Christine had in mind for a romantic conception ritual. She said, somewhat irritated, "Wait! Can we talk about this?"

"Now just listen to this song, and see if it's not perfect." Terry was undaunted by her agitation.

Christine sat in a chair next to the window, trying not to loose her temper. But Terry was suddenly so enthusiastic it was hard to stay angry at him.

"I've never sung this to you, but I wrote it once long before we met. Now just listen." Terry hunched over his guitar, tuning and plucking notes, trying to find the melody. In the bottom of his guitar case were some songs that he hadn't played in years. He shuffled through the pages and found some words scratched out on a piece of paper. "Here it is!" he shouted. "Now listen, Christine."

The name of the tune was "If I Had a Son," It wasn't a Top 10 hit single, but it had a lot of feeling. The second verse started, "If I had a daughter . . ." Christine had forgotten the talent he had. She was also feeling overwhelmed. "Terry, I like your song, but now I feel like this is your ritual, not ours."

He paused, and then said, "Well, what do you want to say to your child?"

She replied thoughtfully, "I would say that we are ready and want you here and we are happy that you are coming into our lives."

"Well, Christine, I'll sing my song and then you say what you want to say. Then we'll both light the candle and make love."

She looked at him, "That sounds good, but first I need to say that I feel angry that you came down so hard on me. I feel hurt."

"I'm sorry I yelled, but I'm not sorry I spoke up. This is important to me, too. I need to feel as much a part of it as you do."

"Well, do you?" Christine looked at him.

"Yes!" He grabbed her and gave her a big kiss. They talked for a few more minutes.

Then Christine said slowly, "Okay, all's forgiven. Let's give it a try."

They sat facing each other on the bed. Then he looked at her and said softly, "I know this is out of order, but I feel I want to light the candle first. Is that okay with you?" She agreed.

Terry lit the candle and passed it from hand to hand around Christine, making a circle of light around her. "I want to begin by blessing your new mother, Little One. She is beautiful and loving and will make a great mom."

Christine was startled and very touched by Terry's words. She took the candle and did the same, saying, "I want to bless your father. He is loving and wise and fun to be with. He will make a great father for you, little child."

Terry took the candle from her gently and set it on the table next to the bed, and he picked up his guitar. He played the song he had written. When he was finished, he took Christine's hand and said in a soft whisper, "We love you already, and we want you to be healthy and happy in your new home."

Christine looked at Terry, she was really moved and very much in love with him.

"Little One," she said, "we bless you coming through us. I want you to know I love you and that we are happy you are coming into our lives. I am ready to be your mother."

Terry was looking at her lovingly. The candle splashed light on the walls as he reached over and gently combed her hair back with his fingers.

Creating Your Own Ritual

Terry and Christine's ritual developed spontaneously from their mutual talents and personalities. Their distinct characters, while creating some friction, eventually brought them closer together.

Sometimes creating rituals can uncover dynamics between people that cause friction. When issues arise it's important to discuss uncomfortable feelings before the ritual starts, being careful to clear any negativity. Because rites are powerful tools of transformation, you want to be sure you are setting a positive and healthy intention before you begin. Here are some guidelines to get you started:

1. Clear uncomfortable feelings.

2. Set your intention together; for example, honoring each other as parents and blessing the child-to-be.

3. Take a look at the elements (earth, air, fire, and water) you are drawn to use; for example, a candle, some water for blessing, a little sage burning in a shell. (Sage smoke has been used for centuries by Native Americans to cleanse the air of negative energy. Cedar can also be burned; it is used by many tribes to invite positive energy into a room.)

4. Perhaps you have a favorite poem or song to share. Remember to keep it simple.

In a conception ritual, you don't need a lot of elaboration—making love is a rite in itself.

4
Birth: Preparing for Your Baby

Colina Azul

Your mother is as round
as the green hills.
We will name you for the hills,
We will name you for the blue sky.

A few weeks before the birth of their child, Carlos and Cindy sat to-gether, admiring the work they had done on the baby's room. All of the furniture hadn't arrived yet, but the painting and papering were complete. They had only to purchase a few more items. Cindy turned to Carlos and said, "This seems like a good time to do our little ritual." He smiled in agreement.

He went into the kitchen, turned off the phone, and got a bowl of water. She brought a candle in a bowl of earth collected from the garden. She picked up a packet of sweet pea seeds, the flower of April. They met at the door of the baby's room. He gave her a delicate kiss and they en-tered. Cindy lit the candle.

"Little child," she said, "we already love you and today we have made a place for you. We welcome you into our lives."

Carlos took the water and sprinkled it around the room. "We bless this space and welcome you."

Then Cindy took the candle from the pot of earth and handed the light to Carlos. She drew concentric circles in the dirt with her finger, and sprinkled seeds in the troughs. After Carlos gently covered the seeds and tamped the earth, he poured a little water over the mound. Cindy placed the bowl of soil on the floor in the center of the room.

"They should bloom just about the time you're born, Little One," she said to her belly, softly patting her stomach.

Carlos placed the candle next to the bowl. He reached around Cindy from behind and lifted her tummy, to take pressure off her back. She rested in his arms. They stood together for a long time watching the flame light up the room.

Creating Your Own Ritual

If you want to welcome your baby into the world, what are the most important feelings you have to express to your spouse, to the arriving child, or to the rest of your supportive circle? Are there elements representing growth and new life that have meaning for you? Carlos and Cindy used sweet peas for the month of April. Perhaps you and your spouse want to plant a tree to commemorate your child's arrival. You could also incorporate finishing projects, such as painting the baby's room or buying furniture, into the rite.

Inviting friends or family can also help your transition into your new role as parents. Do they have stories of their own that would be helpful? Maybe your parents will tell the story of your birth.

Sometimes in a ritual of welcoming, there may be some grief as well. This is a momentous time, and life changes a lot when children are born. It is important to honor all of your feelings. People often need to grieve the past before they can take hold of the future.

5
Birth: The Moment of Arrival

Our Family

Stitching our lives together
we have gathered you.
Gathering ancestors around our hearts
we have brought you home.

Jesse rested in the dress she and Dave had made for the occasion. Over the past several months they had worked on it a little every day. Now it was completed and she and Dave admired its beauty as she sat quietly in bed.

She had sewn in pieces of dresses from grandmothers on both sides of the family. There was ribbon from her mother's wedding dress and a little lace from Dave's mom. The men in the family had contributed bits of their favorite neckties. Dave had sewn in a stone that he had from when he was a boy.

It looked a little like an old-fashioned crazy quilt. Everything on the dress had a story to it, weaving the two families together to celebrate their new arrival.

Jesse helped Dave into his new vest. It had belonged to Dave's grandfather. They had sewn onto the vest the same bits and pieces they had used for the dress.

The contractions started to become more regular. Dave lit a candle and looked lovingly at his wife. As a part of their ritual, they washed each other's faces and hands, each blessing the other as soon-to-be parents. He kissed her softly.

Jesse's contractions were ten minutes apart. The two of them sat together, enjoying the closeness they felt just before the birth of their first child.

When the nurse stopped by to check on everything, she took pictures of the two of them. Just after the pictures were taken, the contractions came closer together. Dave helped Jesse out of her dress and into a hospital gown for the delivery.

A few hours later they were in the delivery room with their son,

Jason. Dave was still wearing his vest. He reached in the pocket for a little cap he had made for his son.

Creating Your Own Ritual

The point of this ceremony is to find a way to express your love for one another, honoring each other as new parents, and marking this very important transition in some significant way. If you begin with this intention, you are sure to come up with a loving and meaningful rite of birth.

If neither of you sew, consider asking a relative to help you with your own versions of Dave and Jesse's garments. If this ritual doesn't strike you, consider the following ideas to help you brainstorm:

In a loving way, wash each other's face and hands.

Light a candle and pass it around one another, each telling what you love about the other.

Either on the day of delivery or after the birth, light candles of three different colors representing each one of you. Save the baby's candle for last, lighting it with the two 'parent' candles. You could do this at your last meal together as a couple, or the first meal together as a family.

Find or create poems that express your love to each other.

Brainstorm the preceding idea together, and see what feels right for you. A combination of these suggestions may feel more appropriate.

Don't discount any ideas, even if they sound silly—just write them down. Then go over the list and look at what ideas attract you the most. Rituals are like stories and can have a beginning, middle, and end. Tell the story of your intention, excitement, and love together, and you will have your rite of birth.

Of course, the day of a birth is often chaotic, and full of unexpected twists and turns. However, having someway to honor one another is the main point. Enjoy the ride!

6
A Naming Ceremony

On Your First Day Home

Alisha you began
like the first moments
of a new day,
not completely sure
that you wanted to give up the night.

But you fought your way here
and were encouraged
by your mother's struggle
to bring you home.
You came kicking and howling
with the will of a young wolf.

Today you are strong
and lovely
and whole
in your bright
new
star body.

Barbara and Lincoln had gone through a lot to bring Alisha into this world. She was born premature, and for months before the birth, Barbara was flat on her back in the hospital.

In her sixth month of pregnancy, she was plagued by host of difficulties. Three times a week I went to visit her during her stay in the hospital. I used guided imagery to bring her blood pressure down and her platelet count up. We worked to calm the baby, energize Barbara, and keep her from having the baby too soon.

In her seventh month, Barbara's platelet count was shaky. Her doctor made the decision that it was time to deliver.

Alisha's first few weeks of life were touch-and-go. She fought like a little tiger, but they weren't sure if she would make it. For a month after she was born, Alisha remained in the hospital.

Barbara had recovered well, and although the pregnancy and delivery took their toll on her body, she remained excited to be a full-time mother. Because of conflicting medical opinions about Alisha's future health, Lincoln and Barbara's first month as parents was difficult. But finally Alisha could go home.

Barbara had asked me if we could do a little ritual to celebrate her arrival at her new home. When Alisha woke up from her first nap in her own bed, Barbara and Lincoln gathered her and themselves together. I found a miniature rose in the garden; it was the only flower that was blooming. It seemed to be there just for Alisha. I cut the rose and floated it in a clear glass bowl full of water. I had found a candle shaped like angels with their wings touching, and brought it to the living room coffee table for the occasion. The sun was setting and the moon was rising as we sat in a semicircle around the table. Barbara held tiny Alisha in her arms.

First I lit the candle. It seemed perfect. I said a few words about the angel candle being right for a new beginning. I acknowledged how hard the past several months had been.

"Tonight is the beginning of a new time, a time when the three of you are starting as a family for the first time under one roof." I handed the bowl to Lincoln and asked that he take a little water and bless his daughter, and then his wife. He did so and welcomed each into their new life. Then he handed the bowl to Barbara and she blessed Alisha and Lincoln. Barbara said Alisha's full name as she patted her head with the rose water. After she was done, I took the bowl and blessed all three of them.

"We ask for more peaceful times. We ask that from now on, there be more serenity and harmony surrounding this new family."

We sat for a while in the glow of the candle. Alisha slept in her mother's arms with her tiny fingers gently curled over her blanket.

Creating Your Own Ritual

Hopefully your family will have an easier time than Lincoln and Barbara had bringing a baby into the world. The effect of this ritual for them has been more peace and less chaos in their lives. Since Alisha's arrival home she has grown steadily, and today she is a very happy, healthy, and active three-year-old.

This ritual can be used for several occasions — in naming, in welcoming home, or in blessing, whether the baby is a newborn or a one-year-old. Variations can be used for young children through age five. If the child is adopted, no matter what age, this ritual can provide a way to welcome the child and begin your new life as a family. Young children can enjoy blessing others with the water, as well as receiving the blessing themselves.

In whatever spiritual tradition you prefer, a rose, a candle, and water are simple, meaningful tools for blessing your new arrival. The rose signifies love, budding, blossoming, beauty, and peace. Water represents cleansing, emotion, and flow. In relationship to the earth, water represents the west. Besides providing a focal point to the rite, the candle represents the light of the soul, higher intention, unity, love, and harmony; the yellow of the flame also represents the east—a new beginning.

In Alisha's ritual the rites for birth, welcoming, and naming were done all at once. You can break them up to occur over several weeks, starting before delivery and ending with a naming ceremony.

7
Celebrating the First Adult Action

Welcome

Today you have begun to stand
on your young man legs.

Let this gentle reassurance
take you by the hand.

Jamie was seven. He had done his chores, without anyone asking him to, for the first time. His father, Richard, had noticed this and talked to his wife, Donna. She agreed to create a special meal that night in Jamie's honor.

Donna made Jamie's favorite dinner. Before they began to eat, Richard made an announcement in front of the whole family: "Jamie, today you did your first adult thing—you took the trash out without anyone asking you, and we are celebrating this with your favorite supper. I want to give you something that I've been saving for you."

His father took out a pocketknife that had belonged to him when he was a boy. "I'm giving you this in honor of the day when you have begun to take on responsibility. Grandpa Joe gave me this pocketknife. I want you to understand that it is not to be used to harm another living thing. It is to be used to help you when you're camping or to carve sticks. Is that clear?" Jamie nodded in understanding as his father handed him the knife. The boy's eyes were as big as saucers.

"Why didn't I get one?" Lisa whined. Donna turned to their five-year-old, and said, "When you're a little older and are ready to begin sharing work in the family a little more, we will have a special dinner for you, too."

Lisa seemed to understand, although she didn't like the answer. Jamie was rolling the knife over in his hand, touching the handle as if he had just discovered buried treasure.

Creating Your Own Ritual

In the Northwest Coast cultures of Native America, potlatches or giveaways were bestowed in honor of children's initiation into adulthood as well as other ceremonial events. The child received very little of material value' his or her gift was a spiritual one, namely the honor of becoming an adult member of the community. Not only did the child have to prove their practical skills, they also demonstrated their knowledge of the songs, mythology, and blessings that went alone with food gathering and preparation. The giveaway honors the child while giving directly to the community and redistributing the wealth. The wealth and status of the host was measured by his generosity. Sometimes the host even gave away his house.

It is different in our culture. We give a gift to a person. The individual is honored with the gift. Status is in material value and accumulated wealth.

Keep in mind that giving a gift is a symbolic way to commemorate a moment of crossing into a new time of life. A gift of the heart need not be expensive or linked to status. Handmade gifts can be less expensive and more meaningful.

Maybe you have a daughter Jamie's age. Perhaps she is beginning to help around the house without being asked. Maybe she looked after a neighbor's dog, or helped someone. Perhaps you have something special to give her to mark this day.

What would it be?

8
Adolescent Passages and Sexual Identity

Earth as Mother

I lay like an infant
in the grass belly down,
pour out my pain, anger, fear.
Only I can let it go
only she can take it away.
I stretch my arms wide to embrace her
sun warming my back
and whisper thank you,
thank you,
through my tears.

Adolescent rites of passage hold the most profound changes we can make for the futures of young people now and for proceeding generations. When a child is initiated into adulthood, they are acknowledged for who they are no matter what gender, no matter their educational ambitions, and no matter their race, or religion. The seeds of adulthood begin to blossom in them. I have seen this in my own family, I have witnessed it from stories that have been told to me, and I have experienced enough initiation myself to know that this is true for any rite of passage, no matter the age of the person.

Rites for adolescents can be given today to children without practices that would be considered barbaric in contemporary society. Of course there are many people of all ages that have gotten tattoos as a way to celebrate passages. So perhaps we are not so far away from such practices as we moderns might think.

Rites such as circumcision was and is practiced in certain religious contexts such as in Judaism and it is practiced in a medical context because it is thought to be healthier for boys in their self-care and disease transmission. Genital mutilation for women is considered abusive by many people, especially in the United States, and is seen as a way to make women subservient to men. Blood-letting in contemporary society is not accepted and would not be considered as a practice that most people, especially those in Western civilization, could accept. I am not addressing rites that mutilate or harm because they are not necessary in our current culture. None of these ceremonies are meant to manipulate anyone else, as some practices do in Earth-based traditions such as Voo-doo, or some forms of Santaria. My sole intention is to empower individuals being initiated rather than disempowering them or offering harm producing tools.

Currently we have rites that acknowledge the intellectual development of a person, such as graduations from Middle School, High School or college. With regard to gender roles, and acknowledging who we are as a unique ray of light, there has been much change since the 1960's. Prior to the last sixty years, western men and women were tracked to be in roles that were fairly strict through traditions of confirmation and marriage rites.

When I was growing up in the 60's my parents formed a marriage and became two halves of a whole primarily to raise children. The male was the bread-winner, and the woman was the queen of the household bearing children and keeping track of relationship dynamics. Even today in traditional religions, women and men are married with this in mind. However, since the 60's, most women today are permanently out of the box of the patriarchy. There is nothing that will turn the clock back, nor will most young women and men that I know of today even consider such restrictive life scenarios. Sexual roles and identities are changing and there is a need to change them for more authentic personal expression as well as economic well-being. Both women and men have more choices in how they are going to make their way in the world.

What has not been often acknowledged in women's liberation is that men have been liberated too. No longer do they need to be locked in old roles of money making and work in the same ways. Many men choose to stay home with the kids, and be the primary care giver while their more ambitious wives go off to work. Beyond economics, something else is happening. Women have had to develop their masculine energy more internally to be in the world outside the home. Men have the opportunity to grow their feminine and stay home with the kids if they want to. Those who are not strictly female or male, but are a blend of genders are more accepted today as the reality in a much broader spectrum of sexual expression between macho men, and highly feminine women. Any gender variations in the past were not acknowledged but hidden or shunned. To acknowledge sexual variation is a very new phenomena in the last 50 years, not only to acknowledge the range of sexual variety, but also to honor it!

Unfortunately, in most countries in the world, we are not there yet.

As the economic climate has worsened in the U.S. and Europe, both men and women need to work to support their families. In poor families as well as wealthier families the economics keep both genders working and often too little attention is paid to the children. This is one reason that offering children a rite of passage helps refocus families towards their teenagers rather than away from them.

A rite of passage does not happen in a vacuum, it happens in a familial context of relating that is already established. It gives everyone a chance to stop and reflect on the previous years and sets a tone towards improving communication to get through the teenage years. A rite of passage also supports children to feel loved and connected when most children in their early teens feel more insecure and challenged as they pass through junior high or high school. Today we have an opportunity to create a rite that is tailor made for the child no matter their interests or sexual orientation.

As a side note, strict roles in families have not been the norm for all cultures. In many Native American ceremonies that I have been a part of, I learned how different roles for men and women were traditionally more fluid in the old days. All people of various genders were honored for their variation. This at least has been true in Lakota Sioux nation and in various other tribal groups throughout the west and the Southwest. In some cases, they were give roles that evolved out of their purpose for being that were given through their naming rituals done before or just after birth.6

Homosexual men or women were thought to be holy women and men, and they were often given titles that reflected their unique perspectives. Some of them became shamans, Hayokas, or backwards people, who taught about joy and death in ceremonies and rituals. Some brought information from the spirit world, to share with the community; shamans were able to move from one world to another to bring information back from the other world, to inform this one.

This is not to say that women did not have roles and gender-based tasks such as gathering and preparing food, and men had tasks such as gathering wood and hunting that helped them identify their separate roles, physical abilities, and identities. However both men and women knew how to do everything, as this was a more practical way for them to survive. Women knew how to hunt and men knew how to cook. It made sense, especially when men went off on raiding parties or were off fighting other tribes.

33

All this is to say we can be influenced by healthier examples of the past to create a new world order that seems to be striving to acknowledge people where they are, rather than what has been defined by the patriarchy.

The patriarchy is dead and dying. It served a purpose at one time, but there is much that has been revealed in the underbelly of the patriarchy that none of us want anymore, namely sexual abuse of women and children, glass ceilings that won't allow well qualified women to advance, and more good old boys clubs that lock out anyone who challenges certain white male dominated realms. However, it is not quite clear what is forming yet to move beyond these antiquated 'norms.'

Perhaps what we are developing next is a humanarcy rather than matriarchy or patriarchy. Wouldn't it be wonderful if the qualities of a person and what they had to offer were more important than gender specific roles? We are trending in that direction.

There are uses for these roles when raising children, but they do not have to be strictly followed. A rite of passage can support a child in all their uniqueness and beauty to become contributing adults with all their gifts and talents.

There are specific ways that initiation can support the development of both men and women. For example, it is true that work and initiation for men are closely tied together. As women become more integrated into the workforce they will also need new rites to help them maintain their femininity and grow their sense of self as they work as well. As women take up work, they also are taking on more political appointments to change the very male dominated culture of the past for the good of all people.

Psychologically, men need to separate from their mothers and identify with their fathers to become men as they enter their teen years from ages 11-14. Men and women are different. We need new ways for men and women to acknowledge their desires and needs. At the same time it is important for men to acknowledge where they come from and stay in respectful relationships with their mothers while forming their male identity. Women also need to respect and look up to their fathers. However, with so many absent fathers or disenfranchised families this relationship is often strained or non-existent. Rites of passage can help girls and boys enter adulthood like nothing else we have invented in societies.

For girls, initiation does come naturally with menses, marriage and childbirth, when women become mothers and their priorities change irrevocably. They see that their actions affect another life. Mature men see

34

the same thing when they hold their newborns. Some run from this responsibility, others engage it.

We need to find ways to initiate boys into manhood and girls into womanhood because adolescence is extended by too many youth into their twenties. Our 2008 financial crisis points to the reasons why passages would help make better men and women. One of the most widely quoted statement by a Wall Street executive investing other people's money in worthless investments was "We were waiting for the grown-ups to show up and put a stop to it but no one did."

In *The Power of Myth* with Bill Moyers, there is a telling passage:

Moyers: "…given the absence of initiation rituals, which have largely disappeared from our society, the world of imagination as projected on that screen serves, even if in a faulty way, to tell that story doesn't it?"

Campbell: "Yes, but what is unfortunate for us is that a lot of the people who write these stories do not have the sense of their responsibility. These stories are making and breaking lives. But the movies are made up simply to make money. The kind of responsibility that goes into a priesthood with a ritual is not there. That is one of our problems today. …So the youngsters invent (rituals) themselves and you have these raiding gangs, and so forth—that is self-rendered initiation. …A ritual is the enactment of a myth. By participating in a ritual, you are participating in a myth."7

One of our most serious problems today is that we have a society full of uninitiated men who do not take responsibility for their actions and feel that making lots of money is their only initiation. Witness men like Bernie Madoff or the traders who cheated so many out of their retirement funds who have yet to be convicted of any crimes. They never thought of themselves in relationship to society as a whole or the effect that their greedy actions have had on others. They are not surrendered to serve anyone or to a social order that holds standards of behavior. As they knowingly stole money from thousands of people's retirement accounts, they damaged the culture at large. It has harmed the economy by forcing older folks to work longer than they wanted to, and does not allow the younger people into the American dream as these jobs are kept by older people longer because they are not able to let go into their "golden years." As jobs change with new technologies, people with less skill no longer have the apprenticeships they used to pass from father to son a generation or two ago. Instead, we have whole sectors of the economy that cannot find work.

Work and initiation for men are closely tied together, as they stem from these time honored father-son relationships that developed around work centuries ago. The greed continues as wages have not risen with corporate profits except at the highest levels.

Campbell goes onto say:

"...in primary cultures today the girl becomes a woman with her first menstruation. It happens to her. Nature does it to her. And so she has undergone the transformation, and what is her initiation? Typically it is to sit in a little hut for a certain number of days and realize what she is. She sits there. She is now a woman. And what is a woman? A woman is a vehicle of life. Life has overtaken her. Women is what it is all about—the giving of birth and the giving of nourishment. She is identical with the earth goddess in her powers, and she has got to realize that about herself. The boy does not have a happening of this kind, so he has to be turned into a man and voluntarily become a servant of something greater than himself.[8]

Girls become women by being with their creative capacity as a vehicle of life. (Today this does not only mean childbirth necessarily, but can reference her creative capacities.) Boys become men by surrendering to other men (or adults) through initiation, and voluntarily becoming a servant of something greater than himself. Both girls and boys need to realize their creative capacity and become servants of something greater than themselves to reconnect them to the Earth and to others in society as well as to their unique life purpose. It could help girls realize that they are sacred because they are the Mother Earth Goddess, and boys coming to serve the Earth because they are too connected to her intrinsically as protector and supporter. There are dozens of stories about men as gods through Orixas or spirits of nature that can help men define themselves as valuable to support the culture.

Mostly, men in contemporary society need to become more humble to serve the greater good, rather than only themselves by amassing more money and power.

This concept is confirmed in an article by Susan L. Ross, Ph.D.[9] Ross has discovered through interviews with women who travel and receive transformative experiences, that they experience the heroes journey as outlined by Campbell, and Arnold Van Gennep, (more on his work in Chapter Nine) namely; seed idea (Ross), separation (VanGennep) or departure (Ross), transformation (Van Gennep) or the transformative experience (Ross), and the return (Ross) or integration (Van Gennep).

36

But she goes on to describe that there is an equally challenging journey that women go through upon their return from journeys that are of an initiatory nature. This is a journey that comes from ancient Mesopotamia, and has been described as the Inanna story where Inanna dives into the underworld to visit her dark sister. Ross describes this journey as the integrative cycle, namely: displacement, grief and denial, disorientation, dismemberment, surrender and healing, birth, abundance and creativity, power and integration. She has named these two cycles the hero's journey as the transformative cycle, and heroine's journey as the integrative cycle.10 They make up an upright figure eight in her diagram. Indeed, many men go through this integration after returning from war. Their integrative cycle is not always honored or realized, and they must complete it to become reintegrated into society. We saw this painfully with Vietnam vets, and now we continue to see it with veterans who participated in Dessert Storm, and the Gulf wars in Iraq and Iran (really in all wars). There is also the journey of our lives that does not require travel. Ross concludes:

"…The data indicates that the passage of transformation, of becoming the hero who is a "conscious vehicle" (Campbell, 1968, p. 239) of a boon, is only half complete at the point where scholars have considered the process to end; there exists a hidden half of transformation. Findings show that the process requires not one but two arduous, perilous journeys: one into the heights of what is possible as a transcendent superhuman (the hero's journey) and one into the depths of the limitations of self as an earthly creature (the integration journey). An unexpected finding is that the upper cycle cultivates one's masculine and the lower cycle develops one's feminine; together these rounds form an upright infinity symbol or figure eight that comprises a map of the making of everyday heroes. These journeys facilitate the conception of a new self and death of an outdated one, resulting in transformation—the embodiment of one's wholeness as divine and human, masculine and feminine, individual and group—and the apprehension of the hero within.11

I very much agree with Dr. Ross, in that today we have evolved beyond our parents who were each a half of a whole person, the mother stayed home and took care of the kids, and male went out everyday to work. Today both of us do all of it, male and female alike. We are each living our ordinary heroes journey and consequently we need both kinds of initiation, the transformative cycle, and the integrative cycle of initiation to become whole humans that contribute to society and the reconnection to the Earth as sacred. The outer rituals set the stage for inner transformation.

That is an individual contemporary hero/heroine's journey. It is our new cosmic story.

Recently, I visited Headwaters Outdoor School owned and operated by Tim Corcoran in Mount Shasta, California. He has been initiating young men into manhood for almost 30 years. He takes them out into the wilderness and challenges them to become men by climbing mountains, working around the camp, building shelters, forming a code of ethics to live by and seeking a vision for their lives. He helps them see that their actions matter. He challenges them to work together and support one another through group activities that are designed to also teach them life skills. He most importantly immerses them in the beauty and presence of nature. He helps them feel the earth, their earth, and their connection to it. (see Men's Rites and Rituals-Chapter 10).

Meeting Tim was like meeting an old friend who had been working parallel to my life for our entire adult lives with the same goals. We had been working on the same questions: How do we bring more depth of meaning to Western Culture? How can we bring the depth of meaning we found in Native American Ceremonies to Western culture without exploiting Native Americans or transposing one culture onto another? How can we help heal our relationship with the Earth?

As we spoke, we agreed that reconnecting people to nature is one of the keys to creating transformative rites that matter. Another one is offering people a chance to experience the divine within. While both of us are of European ancestry (Tim is Irish, and I am half Norwegian with Danish/Scottish ancestry), we have both experienced initiations and ceremonies in a deeply personal and direct way in Native American cultures that deeply transformed our lives. I have also experienced Afro-Brazilian cultural traditions in the Umbanda tradition as well. For both of us nature has been, and continues to be, our primary teacher. Mentors who helped with our initiations were also an essential part of who we are today because of their connection to the Earth.

It is why I have asked one of his students, Jonathan, to share his story of initiation as an example of his life changing initiation to showcase his school in this book. These initiations could help to reinvent initiation for men in our society today and will resonate for many more men than he could possibly initiate at Headwaters, though I hope he continues for many years to come with this important work. Both of us agreed that girls and boys both need initiations, male rites and feminine rites. Why? Because, we are evolving from being □ of a whole as in the relationships of old,

38

to being whole within ourselves, and then choosing a partner that is also whole.

Women run a lot of male energy today, working and doing, with little time to be. Men and women need to reflect and find their internal center to feel their feelings, and be with what is in their daily lives. The popularity of meditation today is helping many obtain this calmer center. Going in to be, is awakening the feminine consciousness in all of us.

However, most women do not always grow up honoring their innate intuition, nor the fact of their wisdom. They do not honor their bodies as sacred and do not honor their sexuality with respect. Instead, many girls are encouraged by the culture of commercialism with exploitive over sexualization of their bodies, with fantasies of a perfect wedding and marriage. They are encouraged to diet insanely or disregard their monthly flow as not something that they can honor or need to cleanse their bodies. Wedding dreams are often dashed when the reality of day-to-day life washes over them. So many girls are led to believe that if you look beautiful and have a tiny waist line and large breasts that you will find the perfect man and the perfect life. Some girls don't know that the marriage starts at the wedding and continues day to day. Often they are not told that while economics plays a part, finding a mate who will step-up and take care of the children with you no matter what is a huge issue in today's culture. As couples choose to live together longer, even having children together while not committing to one another or the kids, their lack of commitment harms the children who are often left to themselves.

A vast majority of single parenting is done by women. In the last few decades the statistics have sky-rocketed, and women are often frustrated with adolescent men who refuse to grow up. Men are frustrated with demanding women who they see as 'taking' their money while in actuality they are supporting their children and the women who care for them. According to the U.S. Census Bureau in November, 2009, there are approximately 13.7 million single parents in the United States today, and those parents are responsible for raising 21.8 million children (approximately 26% of children under 21 in the U.S. today). Approximately 84% of custodial parents are mothers, and 16% of custodial parents are fathers.12

While we cannot change the statistics, we can begin to offer our children ways to support transitions and to accept their circumstances. This is where initiation can be essential and fundamentally useful to change dynamics in relationships. We always begin with what is.

In addition today, we have more acceptance of homo-sexuality as a natural phenomena. Our current millennial generation is more accepting of various kinds of 'gender-bending' as one friend called it recently. There are trans-gender, trans-sexual, and otherly gendered people in the world.

This is a reality. No religious dogma is going to wish these people away, though political regimens as well as religious fundamentalists have certainly tried.

Perhaps it is time we found rites that acknowledge who one is as one is, rather than trying to fit into old boxes of orthodoxy or patriarchy. All people never fit into these boxes in the first place. While these "boxes" were at one time to support a community that supported and protected the children with strict moral values that people were to follow, they have not worked to do this in reality in the present day. Acknowledgement and acceptance does work to build the self-esteem and empower each person to find their own place in the culture at large. This I see every day in my private practice.

Culture in the Americas and throughout most of the world is moving towards acceptance of our diversity, NOT a homogeneous one as some would like to impose. If there is to be acceptance of all types of folks, no matter their shape or size, rites of passage are one way to start. At the very least, personal rituals can be ways for differently gendered folks to accept themselves. This is very important and the first step for them to be accepted in the outside world.

One of the main reasons for Ceremonies from the Heart is that we have a very big problem with our culture especially with regards to men and their much needed initiation, especially in light of the quote from a Wall Streeter cited previously. Men and women must accept responsibility for their lives and how they are interconnected to all the rest of the world, including nature and her web of life, if we are to survive in a sustainable world. We must become centered in alignment with the Earth and embedded in the reality that we are nature itself—the Earth is our body—so that we stop treating the Earth as a separate usable commodity that is only good for generating wealth. What we put into or on the Earth, we put into and onto ourselves. This does not mean halting industry or technology, it means changing how we do things in consideration of the Earth. Can we eat it, should become our test of chemical safety. Are we using technology for the Earth with sustainable products? It is also checking our attitude towards the Earth and changing it from one of taking to one of asking with gratitude.

Part of the cultural problem we have stems from how we view our economics. We see our culture is based on money instead of on nature.

The tangled web of the recent financial crisis keeps everyone distracted. But the truth is EVERYTHING is based on nature; economics, food, housing, shelter, clothing, books, magazines, plastics, IPads, cell phones, everything.

As Pulitzer prize-winning author and New York Times financial reporter Gretchen Morgansen said recently on Bill Moyers Live, "I feel like an archeologist finding bits and evidence of what happened [in the financial crisis]…No one wanted anyone to see what really happened [with the banks and morgages]."13

What does the financial crisis have to do with rites of passage? How is cheating people out of their money support a moral ethic for all people? M.B.A. business colleges have responded by stepping up the inclusion of 'ethics" as a required courses.14 Business ethics wained in the 1990's and 2000's and was not even taught to business students in many schools as stated in Morgansen's article. This created a culture of commodification rather than of sustainability and moral integrity. Business schools are stepping up their response to the current crisis by including ethics in business schools and not just as an elective in Philosophy courses, but as required in the business schools at Yale, Stanford, and NYU Stern School of Business, etc.

Could moral ethics change with rites of passage? As Tim Corcoran has developed in Headwaters Outdoor School, the children develop a 'code to live by." My nieces and nephews have stated that their rite of passage was the beginning of thinking how they would live their lives.

While it might not change everything, I think rites of passage could certainly help. It could help to change our relationship from money as the base of our culture to nature as the base of our culture and help us view this reality that seems to be missed by too many! Nature is important to everyone whether they live in cities or not, however, that connection to nature must be felt by the initiate.

The problem is that traditional tribal rites of passage would never fly in our current culture for the masses of people because they were created from a time when people were tougher and hard physical labor was not thought of as passé as it is today. They were also tied to an more agrarian culture where the men are strong and the women were subservient for the most part, but even this is not at all accurate in many tribal cultures.

In many Native American tribal groups, while women and men were honored in different ways, they were still honored equally. It was the women, especially the older women, who had the last word. This is true today as well in many Native American gatherings. Most modern people today, including many thousands of Native Americans, live in cities. Urban life does not foster a true and balanced connection with nature.

It seems to me that humanity is coming into greater awareness that goes beyond the old ways of relating. We are finding new ways of relating to ourselves and to the world. I feel we have to give ourselves the rites that have been lost to time if we did not receive them.

So turning back to adolescent rites and how we can reintroduce and reshape initiation at this time in human story, gender diversity awareness can be acknowledged while we talk about all of the rites and rituals for girls and for boys. Please feel free to use these rites as a starting point for your creative ritual for your child or grandchild no matter what their orientation or diversity. I will be starting with a rite that I created for my family, then move into rites for men, and moving towards rites for both genders and then rites for Womanhood. I hope you enjoy the stories for inspiration for your life passages.

9
Adolescent Rituals for Children Moving Towards Adulthood

The Blue Heron Ceremony
A Ritual for All Adolecents

The Great Blue

Herons hide in full view.
They know how to draw
the land around them.
They know how to blend
and when to let the light
stream over their imperfect feathers.

The front door blew open and the Michigan contingent blew in. Lysne and I walked in, with her parents Sidney and Kisti and their boys, Ben and Nate. The whole family was gathering for the day's activities. We had two important birthdays to celebrate, my father's and my grandmother's. This year, relatives from the West Coast were joining us at my parent's home in Rockford, Illinois, so our Fourth of July was larger and took on a more festive atmosphere than usual. The house was full of people. Our grandparents and a few adults sat in the living room catching up with each other. The children ran in and out of the house playing games. In the kitchen, my sisters and cousins were preparing dishes of baked beans, salads, and desserts. The aroma of baked ham, and turkey filled the air.

As we settled into dinner preparation and greeted those who had already arrived, Mom asked about what we had planned for my niece. I shyly stated to family members, within earshot, that I had something nice for Lysne. All of us could share in the gift and we could do it after dinner sometime. It seemed to satisfy their curiosity and got me off the hook since I wasn't exactly sure what we would be doing.

After dinner we gathered under the oak tree on the patio. There were at least twenty-five adults, with the younger children running in and out of the circle settling on empty laps from time to time.

Not knowing what I would say or how I would begin, I knew I would have the right words to say when the time came to speak. My nerves were just below the surface and I struggled to calm them with long slow breaths. I was not one of the more vocal members of the family. I was afraid to put my ideas and inspirations out in front for criticism or comment. I held on to the gift that I would unwrap when the time was right.

I was relieved when my grandfather, Lysne, began. He was a quiet man who spoke with a soft somewhat raspy voice. Because it was often hard to hear him, he did not always speak up in gatherings. That day, he spoke very clearly and said he had several stories to share. He wanted to tell us while he had the opportunity.

The first was a story about a king, who on the birth of his beautiful daughter commissioned the town tapestry maker to create for his child a tapestry in her honor. The weaver could take as long as he wished to complete the gift, however it had to be presented on her wedding day. The man agreed, and set out that very day to begin the tapestry. On the princess's wedding day, some 20 years later, the craftsman delivered the tapestry to the palace. The king was overjoyed with the work and summoned the weaver to his court. His Majesty proclaimed that the craftsman could have anything he wished from the kingdom. After a long time, the man said to the king, "Your Highness, all I desire is to see the front of the tapestry." Surprised, the king ordered the tapestry to be brought into the court and it was unrolled for the weaver and his family to see.

Grandpa said that looking around the circle, he felt like the tapestry weaver who could finally see the fruits of his labors. Four generations were gathered that day. His story gave us a sense of being part of the tapestry. I was touched at the loving way he presented the story.

In the second story, Grandpa told us of the origins of the Lysne name. The name was my grandfather's surname, my mother's maiden name. Our people had come from the Sogne Fjord in Norway. The Lysne's were the people who lived at the top of the mountains at the end of the fjord. They signaled the people in town of approaching ships with a horn. As the sun rose in the east, their homes were the first to be illuminated by the rising sun. They became known as "Light," or "Lysne, becoming light."

44

None of us had heard the story of our family name before. We were all well aware of the profound gift that Grandpa was giving us. Many had been restless at the beginning of his story, but now we knew he was giving us something very important. He continued to speak of his childhood and the horn that he remembered on the fireplace mantle of his childhood home in northern Wisconsin.

Grandpa had cleared the way. The stories had made the ceremony unfold exquisitely. At that moment, I experienced a profound connection to my family as well as my Norwegian ancestors.

My turn was next. I was sitting in the presence of my loved ones. I wanted the event to have meaning for all of us, which was a challenge because we are a family of rather eclectic spiritual beliefs. Some are Buddhist, Baptist, Jewish and Lutheran, others are avid students of metaphysics or combine a variety of practices to suit their understanding of the Universe. I did not want to offend anyone. I said a prayer and began to speak.

"We are gathered to honor an important time in Lysne's life. She is the first grandchild in the family and I want to celebrate her passage into adulthood in a special way."

I unwrapped the wooden bird with feathers around its neck that I had carved. I told them how my sister-in-law had given me Great Blue Heron Feathers that hung around its neck. Since our surname was "Heerens", pronounced like the bird, it seemed the feathers and the bird belonged to the family. I shared with them that in the reading I had done on some traditional native African ceremonies, there are often makers of the ceremonial objects and the keepers of those objects. (Film: "The Art of the Dogon", North Africa.) For my father's birthday, I wanted to honor him by making him the keeper of the Blue Heron. (In truth, it was an honor bestowed on both my parents.)

I asked each person to take the bird from Lysne and bless her in some way, either silently or openly. Then after receiving the blessing, Lysne would take the bird and pass it to the next person, proceeding around the circle. Then I said, "Lysne is an important person in my life. She has a kind of wisdom unusual for her age. She has the grace and beauty of the heron. As the first grandchild in the family, her name will always be hidden within the feathers of the bird. The blue of the feathers is not true pigment, it is reflected light." Grandpa's story of the Lysne name had brought a richness to the event in a way that none of us could have guessed.

I tearfully gave the bird to Lysne and she proceeded around the circle from person to person. Feelings were shared and tears began to fall as we realized what a gift she had been to all of us. Lysne had a chance to hear her unique qualities affirmed that were now her responsibility to cultivate or change.

When Lysne completed the circle, I rose and hugged her. I silently said a little prayer of thanksgiving for the day and my family and for the great blue heron. As she handed me the sculpture, I asked that this be the first of a tradition of Blue Heron ceremonies that take place to honor the children in the family. At the time of the thirteenth birthdays, or as soon after their birthdays as we could manage, a ceremony in honor of each of the nine grandchildren would take place. I presented the bird to my father as the keeper of the blue heron. The ceremony was over. The feathers had found their place.

I realized that my nervousness and fears of offending someone were not as important as the love we shared. My family gathered together with the simple understanding that we were going to "do something nice" for Lysne and we discovered a deeper connection to one another than we had known before. This ceremony was not about philosophy, it was about feeling and taking time to share ourselves honestly and openly with one another.

Reflections from the Family. Since that summer, I have had several conversations with various members of the family concerning the ceremony and how it affected them. My sister Kisti told me recently, "It's been one of the most important recognitions for me of something I didn't get as a young person. Through Lysne, I experienced a circle closing." She went on to say that Lysine's ritual became vital for her in another way. The ritual helped Kisti let go of mothering Lysne in the way she had been. Kisti realized that Lysne was now, psychologically at least, her own person. Although Lysne was still Kisti's daughter, they began to establish a new relationship together as well as within themselves.

Five years after her ceremony, Lysne and I drove to California together where I was about to attend graduate school. I asked her to tell me what the ritual had meant to her. After a painfully long silence in which I feared that it had meant nothing to her, she said thoughtfully, "I think for me it was the beginning of looking at what I was going to do with my life. Before that time, I hadn't thought about it much."

Following My Bliss

Shortly after the ritual for Lysne, I began to do more research into rites of passage for adolescents. This was aided in large part by my job, which was Curator of Gallery Exhibits and Museum Outreach and Associate Curator of Art Education at The Ella Sharp Museum, Jackson, Michigan. I was in charge of organizing art exhibits and programming lectures, films or other events pertaining to exhibits. I was also responsible for developing and operating the museum's Arts Go To School Programs. I loved my work and found it to be a constant learning experience.

The Arts Go To School program had three units on Egyptian culture, various American Indian and African cultures for children in fourth, fifth and sixth grades. Volunteers were trained and sent into the classroom with art reproductions, artifacts and books. Through the Arts Go To School program, and the exhibits that I developed for the museum, I learned a great deal about rites and rituals. In order for me to relate the material to groups of children my volunteers were serving, I was constantly looking for information on how and why the masks and objects were used in ceremonies. Most, if not all of the masks had to do with a rite of passage.

The most important aspect of my experiences at the museum was the opportunity to appreciate the paradox of enormous cultural differences in our world, against human realities, which are the same world wide. Everyone has a mother and a father, we all have to grow up, we need food, clothing and shelter, and love. Yet the customs we have to express ourselves as humans varies widely. I wasn't sure how this realization would shape mythic work in the future, but I knew it was important for me as I continued on my way.

Blue Heron II

The second Blue Heron Ceremony took place five years after Lysne's ceremony. Ben, Lysne's brother, had turned thirteen in November. We had planned a vacation in Florida, which would include everyone from my immediate family, my aunt and my grandmother. It was the first time in several years that we would all be together.

My grandmother Lysne was getting more frail; we sensed that it might be her last Christmas. Grandpa had died seven months after Lysne's ceremony. The memory of his stories at the first Blue Heron ceremony had become even more precious to us.

Other changes had taken place in the family. I was divorced and living on my own. There were major shifts in my career as well. I had left the museum, and was making plans to return to graduate school. My younger sister was experiencing strenuous times in her marriage. Another sister had undergone breast surgery to remove malignant tumors. This vacation was a time for all of us to stop and reassess the last few tumultuous years.

Primarily, it was difficult for me to let go of concerns and expectations for the event and Ben. I was more apprehensive about Ben's ceremony than I had been with Lysne's. I wanted this ceremony to work as well for Ben as it had for Lysne. I had been reading more about rituals, and now I knew that in every culture I'd read about, girls and boys had separate rituals. Given this information, I was concerned about how effective the ritual would be for Ben as a boy. Because the ritual for Lysne was largely spontaneous and designed with her in mind, I wasn't sure if it would translate to Ben's needs. I wanted to retain the spontaneity for Ben, and most of all I didn't want any dogma to set in. The old clichés "ignorance is bliss" and "a little bit of knowledge is dangerous", were beginning to make sense to me.

I also had some doubt as to whether the ritual would happen at all. Our family has a tendency to be so relaxed on vacation that plans simply fall together or they don't happen. Any attempt to organize or coordinate anything is sometimes resented. Ben's ceremony got postponed till the last evening we were together. I was greatly relieved when we began in earnest. After dinner, and a birthday party for another nephew, Tyler, my father began with a few words about the ceremony and the reason we were all gathered together.

Ben was sitting reluctantly in a chair besides his grandfather with 2 balloons under his shirt, a party favor in his mouth and a party hat on his forehead like the horn of a unicorn. He looked like some odd mythical beast as he squirmed and wiggled in his chair. The humorous way he sat reminded me that he was very much a boy of thirteen. All the children were high on ice-cream and cake and Ben had eaten more than his share.

My father handled the situation beautifully. He explained the importance of the day. We were gathered together to honor Ben. We were welcoming him into adulthood. It was a time for him to put away childish ways, and begin to see himself as a member of the adult community. He proceeded to ask Ben to remove the paraphernalia and to take the Blue Heron to each member of the family so they could give him a few words.

Ben sheepishly removed the balloons, the hat and the party favor. It struck me how symbolically he was choosing to strip away his former self. He was voluntarily entering into a new phase of his life. He was choosing to transform. He understood that this was a significant event for him.

It struck me how similar Ben's actions were to the ceremonies I had read about with the Massai of Kenya. After circumcision, boys dressed as women before the completion of their rite of passage. Then as they proceeded through the ceremonies, they stripped themselves of feminine clothes to prepare for the final initiations that would transform them into men."15 Their actions separated them from the women in their tribe and began their lives as men. Ben was naturally doing the same thing.

Ben gave the bird to each person in the circle. Everyone had a chance to think about what they wanted to say to him. The advice and blessings he received were for him alone and different than the blessings for Lysne. The comments were unique not only because he was a boy, but because he was Ben.

Another surprise unfolded as Ben passed the bird from person to person. His sister Lysne, having passed through the ceremony, had the privilege of joining the adults in giving Ben the benefit of her years of experience. She spoke to him clearly and resolutely, "Ben, it's not easy growing up. High School was hard, but there are a lot of good parts too, and I know if I did it, you can, too." It became clear to everyone that the younger children were not to speak, only to listen. I was amazed how a natural order arose from what seemed apparent to all of us. My anxiety about the ceremony meeting their needs, disappeared as I watched it progress. At the closing of the circle, I announced that the Blue Heron Ceremony was now a tradition.

I was profoundly moved at how each event unfolded perfectly for Ben and for Lysne without any dictatorial manipulation. There was room for spontaneity within the framework of the rituals. Both Lysne and Ben brought their own unique contributions and needs to each of their ceremonies. The members of the family who participated made each ritual an entirely different event from the previous one. By focusing on the individual rather than gender, the rituals became venues through which all aspects of the child's character and abilities could shine. I was glad I had let go and just enjoyed the event.

Throughout the ceremony, we continued to notice changes from Lysne's ritual. We felt the tension that existed between my sister and her husband. We knew that by the time of the next Blue Heron Ceremony, Grandma would probably not be with us. The health of my sister was uncertain as it might be for any of us. It was a time of profound reflection, mourning and celebration. We felt our connections to one another and to the flow and uncertainty of life. By honoring one, we were in truth honoring and acknowledging all of us. I felt enormously blessed.

New Adventures Experiencing Rites and Rituals.

After Ben's ceremony, I attended graduate school. The Institute in Culture and Creation Spirituality, at Holy Names College, Oakland, California, where I continued working in the area of rites of passage for adolescents, and carried on my research, both academically and experientially. I studied many different traditional rites and rituals and created rites for adolescents in a variety of settings, including a school in Iowa, and a confirmation class in Tiburon, California. I put myself through as many initiating experiences as I could, including Native American sweat lodges, Hanbleceya (known as vision quest to non-native Americans, and traditionally done only by men), and two different traditional woman's ceremonies.

The research and experiences I went through were not meant to contribute to a comprehensive text on rites of passage or to analyze rituals anthropologically. I needed the experiences for my own growth. At the same time, I studied those rites to find ways to create rituals that would work for other people. I wanted the results to be simple enough to translate cross culturally for individuals. Although I could not presume that what held meaning for me would for others, there seemed to be universal aspects of life that everyone needs to nourish their souls. Those aspects are namely to give and receive love, to be acknowledged and to have meaning in life.

The rituals I experienced were guided by my intuition, love, and the need for meaningful experiences like the Blue Heron ceremony. As a result my soul felt nourished. I began by creating a context for myself and my family where we could speak to each other from the heart. We are a microcosm of the society at large, and what worked in our eclectic clan just might work for other people, no matter what their religious or cultural background.

Researching Rites and Rituals

During graduate school, the question of men and women's separate rituals kept haunting me, even though I knew through experience that the Blue Heron Ceremony worked. Around this time I came across a passage that summarized my research and articulated an aspect of what I was thinking:

"Nature initiates women, society initiates men."

Joseph Campbell 16

Through the writing of Campbell, Gennep, Margaret Mead, Mircea

Eliade and others who have studied rites and rituals, I confirmed that in most cultures that have adolescent rituals, boys and girls were given different ones. In general, girls were initiated when they begin menses. Their ability to bear children connected them physically, emotionally, mentally and spiritually to their relatives and ancestors. Boys, on the other hand, needed a ritual to separate them from their mothers on reaching puberty and establish themselves as men, with other men as role models to bring them back into the culture to be of service. They needed tests and challenges from the men in their culture to develop themselves as contributing members of society.

As I read the anthropological studies done of various tribal cultures, I was disturbed, because in most cases, the rituals were being seen by western eyes with western values. Many of the studies were done in the early part of our century shortly after a time when whites destroyed Native American Cultures in the U.S. The hypocrisy enraged me. How could anthropologists from western cultures evaluate rituals in foreign lands when they looked through a cultural lens that portrayed nature and women as the less than men? The societies examined (and destroyed in the U.S.) regarded humans as part of nature and in some cases truly honored women. This was a major philosophical difference. In addition, many of the studies were done by men who had little or no access to women's secret rites.

Even Margaret Mead, one of the most famous anthropologists, who studied passages in indigenous cultures in her books, *Coming of Age in Somoa, Growing Up in New Guinea, Sex and Temperament* gave as accurate accounts as any, but her assumptions of her own cultural differences to the people she studied were not really acknowledged.

Cultures have their own secrets. One friend from Somoa, told me that when Margaret Mead interviewed her grandmother, that they kept much from her, and told stories that were not part of their lives, to keep sacred and secret their own rites from study.

From my viewpoint, one is always experiencing one's surroundings from our own cultural frame of reference. Any experience one might have in a foreign environment is circumspect at best. I draw this from my own experiences on the reservation. Even after ten years, if I did not live on the reservation, I could not understand some cultural details that were available only if I surrendered to the culture as my culture.

However, becoming part of the culture means experiencing subjectively, and scientific studies are not about experiencing as much as they are about observing. Also, I often found that many rituals from other cultures simply couldn't be applied or translated to contemporary western culture.

Some of the studies were outdated, and new up-to-date views were not always available. Some of the cultures researched were not the same due to the encroachment of western technology. It made me realize that whether I wanted to admit it or not I had a "cultural lens" too, and was as much a product of my time as Van Gennep, Mead, or Joseph Campbell.

To add to the confusion, the recent changes in western values especially concerning women's rights, have evolved so rapidly that texts that addressed more equal views of women were not to be found. I often felt confused and at a loss as to how or what I could draw upon to create new rituals.

Nevertheless, as I waded through the quagmire of sexism and racism apparent in the literature, I read several books that helped me understand the vastness of the topic I was attempting to grasp. Observation did reap some benefits for me. A book written in 1906 by Arnold Van Gennep called "The Rites of Passage",[17] outlined several basics for me. He coined the phrase "rites of passage" and made many important contributions to the study of rites and rituals. Although I appreciated Van Gennep's view points, he was a product of his time and culture, and his views were limited by biases that do not honor men and women equally.[18] As an example, p 69, Van Gennep assumes that certain rites after the first appearance of a woman's menstrual flow "are due as much to the impurity of women as to her menstrual flow." It is not at all clear in the text whether this is in fact true of some cultures, or his own opinion. His corroborating examples from the Golden Bough, which is a book of ancient Roman rites, where many western views of women were first to give birth, did not speak from a liberated view point more common today.

A Roman's view would have little to do with an African or New Guinea perspective, also used as examples of other points on the same page. One of the interesting views of Van Gennep differentiated rites of passage from social or physical puberty rites, stating that a rite of passage was needed at a crisis in a person's life, moving from one age group to another, or one stage of life to another. For an adolescent this may occur at any time he or she realizes self-responsibility. Puberty rites had to do with cultural or religious customs around circumcision (many African cultures circumcise boys at the beginning of adolescence), physical changes for either sex, and the first menses for girls.

Perhaps his most valuable contribution was how he delineated three stages which occur in any ritual; separation, transition, and incorporation. Rites of passage for adolescents has a different measure of the three stages than that of other rituals, for example, a funeral rite. In an adolescent rite, separation may be the initial phase while transition and incorporation take place during the majority of the ritual. A funeral may emphasis separation and transition through mourning and the funeral rite, while incorporation may be dealt with at the end of the funeral in the form of prayers or offerings for the soul of the deceased, or mourning which may go on for a long time after the ceremony. He called these phases "schema", which translates as "pattern", "dynamics", "process" or "structure"19, which are very different interpretations in English. However, as I thought about the rituals that I had created, I could identify the parts he delineated.

In the Blue Heron Ceremony, separation occurs as the child is singled out as the recipient of the ritual, transition and incorporation take place during the body of the ritual. Incorporation is most pronounced at the end of the rite when the newly born young adult is applauded and congratulated by the entire family. His writing made sense to me. His work helped me analyze what I had been doing intuitively.

Reflecting on Our Culture

The reading prompted me to think about how different children are today from tribal children living off the land. I learned that generally in tribal groups, kids grew up learning alongside their parents. They took on responsibility gradually for themselves and their clan as part of an extended family, remaining in close daily contact with family members and living integrally with nature for their entire lives. Men and women grew into defined roles, which incorporated limits, taboos and customs. Individual development was important only in the context of the group and how survival would be enhanced. Although I liked the way children learned and how some tribes honored transitions, I realized that going back to the tribe wouldn't solve our cultural decay.

I thought about how much our society had changed since the turn of the century. In my grandmother's time, people lived close to the land, and had large families to support the work that had to be done. From my experience today, we move around following our jobs, developing our careers. Most people are busy making money, trying to get ahead. Families are smaller. We have more leisure time. Factors such as the women's movement and the civil rights movement are beginning to redefine age old constraints of race and roles. Both sexes are able to contribute to culture in whatever way they choose today, with much less resistance than in previous decades. Although the struggle goes on and is by no means over, we have added new stresses and need new ways to honor the changes we go through.

As I continued to look at our society, I saw many people suffering from isolation. We lack connection with one another. Human beings, as part of the natural world, depend on relationships for survival. Because we move around so much, we hardly know our neighbors, let alone develop any sense of continuity from one generation to the other.

Most people are out of touch with nature in the same way we have also lost connection with each other. Because most people today live in the cities as opposed to farms as they did one hundred years ago, we do not have a feeling for the land, which feeds our souls as well as our bodies. In fact the earth is treated as expendable. As the earth suffers, we suffer too.

As a result of the isolation, many families have become fragmented, to the point that some kids hardly know their grandparents, others barely know their parents. Children today aren't ready to be on their own until they are in their twenties. It seemed to me that because of the fragmentation and complexity of our culture, it takes longer for kids to learn what it means to grow up and how to survive.

It didn't surprise me to learn that many kids turn to drugs and commit suicide. Some kids find their initiations joining gangs, or selling drugs. No wonder abuse in families is rampant, the stress in our culture is too great. In the light of my observations and the reading, I concluded that we live in a very fractured stressful society.

Bringing Experience and Research Together

As I thought about how little we consciously offer children in the way of rituals, I had to acknowledge that kids were not getting what they need for their transition into adulthood because we didn't get it ourselves. Creating rituals in our families could help us give a legacy to our children. Through honoring one another, we respect the changing individual within the context of the ever-changing world. By affirming life as it is expressed in each of us, one by one, we acknowledge the changes the culture has made as a whole.

I discovered for myself what seemed to make a ritual work for me, and those for whom I created rituals. From my point of view rituals were effective when those involved felt different about themselves after the initiation, and internalized the transformation, acknowledgements, discoveries or releases that took place as a result of participating. Other ways that I have measured the effectiveness of a ritual has been to ask if there was meaning for people. If the ritual centered around one person making a transition to a new age group, or phase of their life, did they feel as though they had just crossed a threshold to a new way of being in the world? Did they feel more connected to others involved in the ritual? Most of the time I didn't need to ask, I just looked around to see the smiles and knowing looks on everyone's faces.

I decided that I could make sure the kids in my family would have a meaningful ritual for their rite of passage into adulthood. The more I thought about it, the more I realized the significance of the Blue Heron Ceremony. Our family places the emphasis in the Blue Heron ritual on the value of the whole person, rather than defining the individual only by sex. It seems to reflect the changes our culture is making as a whole.

In future Blue Heron Ceremonies, we could validate sexuality in and around the ritual as adults speak about what it means to be a woman or man. Afterwards the child could be recognized by the same sex parent with a special dinner, camp out or trip. The men can create further rituals for the young men around their sexuality, as the girls can be honored by women. However, my family as a whole could honor the boys and the girls as human beings, and that would suffice. Indeed it would be far more than most kids got.

Nathan's Ritual

Two years after Ben's initiation, Nathan (Nate) was turning thirteen. Ben's younger brother was quieter and less gregarious than Ben. His talents were many and he used them masterfully when they were necessary. He was also restrained about expressing his abilities in front of other people. I was curious how his ritual would differ from Ben's and how Nathan's character and other family members who participated, would shape the ceremony.

Christmas took place at my sister Jill's home in Iowa that year. It was cold very outside, snow covered everything. The weather outside seemed to reflect the family mood and energy level.

I was now living in California after finishing graduate school. It was strange for me to be back in the Midwest. The winters seemed colder than I had remembered. Perhaps the loss of our Grandma made this winter feel particularly icy. She had died in February after a long illness. Jill's family had moved to Iowa City from northern Iowa and both Jill and her husband had begun new jobs. My younger sister was now divorced. Other members of the family were struggling with work, school and jobs. I had finished school and was working in an administrative job while establishing a practice in massage. My father had just retired from forty years of medical practice. My mom was adjusting to having Dad around full time. Dad was adjusting to being home and they were both enjoying traveling more often.

Fewer family members were able to attend this gathering. Somehow the smaller numbers and low-key atmosphere seemed to suit Nate's quieter character.

After dinner and an exchange of gifts, we cleared the living room of wrapping paper and gathered everyone. Dad began with the blue heron, announcing that it was Nate's turn to be acknowledged. He said a few words to Nate and gave the bird to him. Nate then passed it from person to person. That day, Nathan was recognized as a gentle and sensitive person with a lot of artistic talent. My mother reminded us that ever since Nate was a small boy, he had bought presents for Christmas with his own money. Some-times it was a rhinestone ring for his grandmother, or a watch for Grandpa, or a hair clip for his mom. Whatever he could spend, he would empty his piggybank. Others noted Nate's sense of humor or his inner strength. They recalled other stories of when he was younger that demonstrated aspects of his character. Nate seemed to appreciate what was expressed. The third Blue Heron Ceremony again reflected the uniqueness of the child. This time it was a quieter ritual, with no less impact on the family than the other two.

Toby and Laura's Rituals

The rites of passage rituals for Toby and Laura, occurred during the Christmas holiday of 1990. After a great deal of shuffled plans, fourteen family members converged on Winter Park, Colorado, near the home of my youngest sister Sara. We rented a large house at a winter ranch in the Rockies. It was very cold and beautiful with fresh snow and cross-country ski trails everywhere.

Toby's ritual began the day after Christmas, Laura's the following evening. Although the ritual format was the same, the two rituals were very different. Because Toby and I were born on the same day, twenty-four years apart, I had always felt a special connection to him. We shared a love for the arts and anything having to do with Japan. He had studied martial arts and so had I. He was the fourth grandchild and I was the fourth child in my family. Four is a sacred number to Native Americans, representing the four directions the four races of humanity, the four seasons, etc., and I felt a kinship with many of their traditions. I wanted to make Toby's rite of passage different in some way. As we gathered in the living room that night after dinner, I sat next to my Dad so that I would be last to speak to Toby.

My father began. He reminded all of us of the importance of this ritual for our family. He spoke to Toby about his gifts and talents and how proud he was to have him as a grandson. His parents spoke of how unbelievable it was to see him at this age. His mom spoke of what a gift he had been to them. She told him of the gift he would receive from both his parents when they returned home. His father spoke of the conflicts he and Toby had, and how through all of it he wanted Toby to know that he loved him and he knew Toby loved him too. My mother, Toby's grandmother, spoke of the legacy she was passing on to Toby as the next generation. She spoke of how proud she was of him. Toby's uncle and aunts acknowledged his talents, told stories of his birth and growing up. There were hugs and tears as each person spoke from the heart to Toby.

When he handed me the heron, I acknowledged the connections we had, how we both shared artistic talent, as well as our place and number in the family. I presented Toby with a kimono, which had belonged to an old friend of mine who is a Japanese sculptor and potter. I told Toby about Yosuke and his ability, and shared how hard the potter worked, his dedication and focus. I also shared with him Yosuke's humility and generosity. I told Toby that the gift symbolized the wealth of spirit that Yosuke has and that Toby has, and that this is far more important than any material wealth he could ever generate. Toby seemed pleased and delighted by the gift. He tried it on, and it fit him, sort of. We joked about how it was something that would grow with him as he grew.

As my father closed the circle with a few final words, Toby had a chance to speak. He said it felt great to have such praise poured over him, like standing under a water fall. His smile reached from ear to ear and wore the kimono around for the rest of the evening. As kids began to run around again and the circle opened, my father turned to me and said, "This is so important, I wish other families would do this. Joseph Campbell would be proud!"

On the last evening of our stay, accommodations had shifted and we had to move to the main lodge in two different buildings. We held Laura's ceremony in my parents' room, which was smaller than the house we had stayed in. As we settled into bunks and beds and on the floor, Dad opened with a few words about the ritual, and offered a few comments to

Laura about her abilities and gifts. Her father, Ralph, told her of the events that occurred before her birth, how his parents had died in an airplane crash just after she was conceived. He spoke of how hard that time was for him and what joy Laura brought through those dark days after his loss. Her mother told her of how joyful it was for her when she was born, on the first day of Spring! She spoke of Grandma and the other women in the family, and how Laura was part of the feminine strength. Nancy and Ralph gave Laura a ring with a dolphin on it. Laura came to me next. I said that although I didn't know Laura as well as I would like, that I shared a particularly close relationship with Laura's mom, and through her felt Laura was special to me. I told her what I had learned, so far, about being a woman. I recognized her abilities and strengths. I gave her a poncho from South America that had belonged to me. Others shared with her the legacy of strong women that we had in our family. She was no exception, and her strength, as she grew may need to be tempered with compassion and gentleness.

Her Aunt Sara told her about the special connection they shared. She didn't know why exactly, but perhaps it was their place in the family, Sara being the fifth daughter, Laura being the fifth grandchild. She invited Laura to spend some time the next summer with her, and looked forward to the visit. Her aunt Jill spoke of what she had learned watching Laura mature, her uncle told her what fun it was to watch her grow up over the years. Since Laura was the first female child since Lysne to go through the ceremony, there was more emphasis on what it was to be a woman in her ritual. Through the women as well as the men, I felt the strength of our family and felt such gratitude.

After I had returned home to California, I received a note from Laura, which thanked me for the poncho and announced ecstatically the beginning of her menses. I was very happy for her especially because her attitude toward her body was so different than mine had been at her age. I had been embarrassed and wanted to hide it even though I was secretly proud to have started. A few months after I received Laura's note, I heard from my sister Nancy, that her Laura was taken out for lunch on her thirteenth birthday by her Aunt, her mother, and several friends to celebrate the beginning of her menses, or "moon time". I was especially delighted to hear it, and very grateful that the ritual had made a difference for my niece.

Michelle's Tradition

At the first ceremony for Lysne, a cousin from Arizona was present. Michelle, or Mickey as she is known in our family, had enjoyed the ceremony tremendously. As a result she created a ceremony for her daughter who became thirteen in 1985.

Mickey planned a dinner for her daughter including the parents, grandparents on both sides of the family, Robin, her daughter, and herself. At the dinner, Mickey brought a rose with her. She used the metaphor of the unfolding rose to speak about how Robin's life was changing. She said, "Robin, as your life emerges you are like the rose. Right now, your life is like the first unfolding petals. As you grow older, the petals of your life will blossom one by one." She continued to speak about how we continue to unfold throughout our life times.

I found Mickey's story beautiful. She had found her own way to celebrate her daughter's growth. It was a time for Mickey to let go of her daughter as a child and embrace her as an emerging adult. As Mickey told me her story, I became aware that my attempt to heal my adolescent wound had sent a ripple throughout the family in a way that I could never have guessed. I was so grateful that I had listened to my intuition and had taken the risk of creating the Blue Heron Ceremony for my family.

Father's Story

Recently, I told a friend about our family ritual. A few weeks later, he told me his story.

Jack has a beautiful twelve-year-old daughter named Mariana. In the last few months, Jack noticed how much Mariana had changed. She had grown several inches and was beginning to mature. He was feeling that she was moving into her adolescence almost overnight. Before she grew too much more, Jack wanted to give her a sense of the transition she was making.

One evening after dinner, he asked Mariana to build a fire in the fireplace, something he usually did himself. She was challenged by his request and enthusiastically set out to struggle with the fire. After the fire was set, Jack began to tell her that it was important for him to share with her the significance of the transition she was making. He saw that she was becoming a woman, and that soon, she would be able to physically give birth. That astonished him. It also made him want to share how significant that would be for her. He told her thathe respected her as a woman, and saw her more as a friend, although he would still be her Dad.

Mariana sat staring at the fire, listening to her father's words. She was speechless. So was I, after hearing of the love and care Jack was willing to show toward his daughter. He had created a way for a single father to recognize and honor his daughter. I realized it didn't take a large family to make an impact on a child, it only took one caring adult.

A Group Version

Over the course of the last few years, I have shared my story with others interested in creating a ritual for transitions. On one occasion, a small Unitarian Church held a ritual for two graduating senior high students. They used the idea from the Blue Heron Ceremony of passing an object, except they used a Native American clay pot instead of a sculpture. Into the pot they placed good wishes and stories and words of wisdom for each young adult who was graduating from high school. Each person had the opportunity to speak to both young adults.

Heartfelt good wishes were expressed to one another. People involved in the event reported that the time of sharing really bonded the congregation. They decided to establish it as part of a tradition for future graduates.

Each time the ritual has been used it seems to act as a container for deep feelings between friends and family members. It doesn't seem to matter what kind of an object is used, where the ritual is held, or who is present. It doesn't matter the gender of the child, this rite works well for all children. The simple format helps the child stand out. Passing the object from the child to a person and back to the child helps maintain a focus while symbolically weaving people together. The only other requirements are willingness between people to express love and caring, that's all it takes.

Perhaps there is a need for such a rite in your family. Who would be there? Who would be honored? Where would you want to hold the ritual? What kind of object would you use to pass from person to person? How would it look?

10
Honoring Passages
Boys to Manhood

Boy to Man

Oh headstrong
and reckless one,
how will the world tame you?
So your will to be who you are,
serves the greater good?

As stated previously in this book, our society is full of uninitiated men. There are many people who do not have a code of ethics, and do not have a moral center because they have been formed by a belief around money being the most important thing, beyond relationships, beyond love, beyond all other values. Because money is now the means of exchange between people, instead of corn or wheat or cattle at least in Western society, we run the risk of devaluing our humanity as a whole by elevating the commercial over our souls. Men especially suffer from this, as they think their only value is in making money for their families or just for themselves.

In Joseph Campbell's cross-cultural studies work and Robert Bly's rites of passage with men, they both say (as well as psychologists) that men also need to separate from their mothers and identify with their fathers to become men as they enter their teen years from ages 11-14. So many absent fathers in our culture create an unprecedented problem because there is a broken link between fathers and sons. These absent fathers have also abandon their daughters in some cases, which also damages relationships for their futures. 20

While boys need to break from their mothers, and bond more with fathers at ages 11-14, it is important for boys to acknowledge and stay in respect for their mothers while forming their healthy male identity. Women also need to respect their fathers, but with so many absent fathers or disenfranchised families this relationship is often strained or non-existent. Rites can help boys and girls enter adulthood like nothing else we have invented in societies.

Honoring Rites for Boys to Men

Here is Jonathan's story of his rites of passage in Mt. Shasta, California. It offers a view of what a modern day rite, that is based on a traditional rites of passage, can offer a boy. The vision quest is borrowed from Native American tradition practiced by many North American tribes. At the end of the book, I have reference to many other rites of passage schools that offer teens and uninitiated men ways to integrate more closely with their society and with nature.

Rites of Passage for Boys- Jonathan's Story

Journey

Up the steep mountain
a boy scared of his shadow,
Down, returns a man,
embraced and placed.

W e were there for ten days altogether. It was the first time camping without my Dad. I wasn't sure what was going to happen up there. I went up very insecure and not very confident, scared of what was going to happen. I missed my family.

We were being lead by the Headwaters Out Door School based in Mt. Shasta, California. We were camping in the marble mountains in Northern California during July. I was 14, some of the guys were 16, others were 13.

The first day we spent the night where all the cars were, because we had to wait for the horses to take our stuff up to the campsite. The next day we hiked up into the mountains. We had to cross the river, there was a roadblock, and finally we got to our campsite. We didn't really need the tents. We just had them in case there was a storm. It was warm enough so that we were able to sleep outside.

I didn't really have time to miss my family once I got there. They worked you pretty hard. We got up early and took hikes. Part of our experience was nature awareness. One morning, they got us up at 5 or 6 a.m. That morning we went out in the wilderness to learn how to track bears. We saw a mother black and her two cubs. It was so awesome! We were on the edge of a field where the bears usually come to eat berries. It was so worth it to wait in the trees to see them.

But that wasn't the rite of passage. During the rites of passage, that was the third or forth day, we started hiking higher up the mountain. We had a backpack with snacks and water. I had a knife. Our group started at 9 a.m. we got to the top by 11:42. We wanted to go to the top, but there was too much snow. And if we had climbed any further without any equipment we would have probably fallen. It was a decision made by all of us in the group. We had to get back to main camp for dinner by 4. If we hadn't gotten back in time, we would have not gotten dinner. We had made an agreement and we had to keep it. We made it back by 3:55!

At night we had to 'camo-up,' by wearing black and blackening our faces. Then we would sneak up to the counselors sitting by the campfire. The counselors were trying to find you by the light of the fire. You were suppose to get as close as you could without them saying "I see you."

Another night we had a counsel meeting with the camp counselors. Before we went on our solo quest, we made our code to live by. This would help us make our way into the future. Once we wrote it down, we had to share it with the group.

Then on the last night, the 9th night, we went on our single vision quest. We chose a spot on the mountain. I had a spot where there was a little clearing, a large oak tree, a pine tree, and a huge boulder. I stayed on the boulder. You weren't suppose to sleep. This way we could take in what was active in nature all night. Early the first night, a doe walked by, then it stopped by the stone. I ended up talking to this doe for an hour and a half! It was a sharing of experience on Earth. It was surreal. At the end of our conversation, I dipped my head to the doe and she dipped her head back. Then she left. It was a major connection between humans and animals. It was so awesome! Later that night, I got to see a great horned owl swoop down and catch a mouse. I love great horned owls. They are so beautiful. At dawn, I saw a mother grizzly and her cub walk by. I watched them by being very still. It was amazing. At 7 a.m. they sent someone out to tell us to come back to let us know that it was time for breakfast.

I was the only one who stayed up all night. I was shocked that I made it through. There was no fear at all! I was astonished at what happen with animals I saw, and how they truly spoke to me!

I learned later that in the Native American traditions when you see any animal, a deer, an owl or bear on a vision quest, they are sharing with you what the Native People call "medicine," or power. These animals and their qualities become part of your medicine. I didn't really tell anyone until later when I came down, I didn't have a need to. It was only later that I realized this when I heard someone talk about Native American medicine.

There was so much that I got from the vision quest. I got to conquer quite a bit of fear up on the mountain. I had a fear of heights, and I got rid of some of that because of the shear drops of the mountains.

After I came back to the city after being gone for 10 days, I thought WOW THIS IS OVERWHELMING! It was so loud! I had to suppress all my senses like touch, feel, smell, and taste. In the wilderness you could let your senses open up and let things in and experience your surroundings. Even though I was overwhelmed when I came back, I felt more confident, sure that I could pull through. I could be determined and confident about what was ahead. It was definitely life changing!

Creating a Rite of Passage Boys into Men

Making a rite of passage, like Jonathan's, takes some wilderness experience and knowledge, some supportive counselors, uncles or fathers, and a group of kids ready for some adventure. This rite of passage, or one like it, would be ideal for a church group, a group of fathers and sons taking an expedition together, or a family with camping experience.

One of my friends, Craig Balletta, just took his boys camping. He did not know what he was doing really, but just started to wing it. He did start with a clear intention; to give his oldest son a rite of passage.

When he and his sons arrived at the campsite, they lit a fire, and talked about what he wanted to do, and they began to talk about the question: What is a healthy male? They discussed what was healthy, and how men are unhealthy too. They spoke about women and what healthy relationships are with women. (He was currently divorced from the mother of the two boys.) The son, turning 13, was sent out into the woods the next day by himself. He sat by a stream for some hours thinking about his life direction, and how he wanted to be as a man. When he came back, they had another campfire and he shared his vision of himself.

With his next son, a few years later, he organized a river rafting trip, he and male friends and their sons went through class three rapids. By the end, the men realized they all had to work together and join forces to get through the rapids together. The difference of the two boys ceremonies, reflected the differences between the brothers. Here is a quote from Craig about his experience with his two sons.

" In both cases it seemed that the intention in my heart to give something to my boys that I did not have and the determination to get into the woods to do it seemed to set the magic and medicine of nature in motion. I had been quite estranged from my father. So I always felt like I was reaching for something that I could not see but must be in reach when I did my best to be 'masculine' for my boys. Nature made it easy. Nature showed up with deer and snakes and bears and cliff jumps and rapids and trees to sit under. I got initiated too."

Direct experience in nature seems to support confidence, awareness and important lessons for personal growth not only for the boys but for the men. It can work for, girls21 too, or otherly gendered. So leave the camper behind and tent up! Maybe if you are in an area like the Marble Mountains, you won't even need tents!

Vision Quest

Vision quests, are ways for people of all ages to get a sense of their purpose for living. A traditional quest requires a lot of preparation. Prayers, intentions, and some form of support, friends, family or people willing to offer a place where a fire can be kept all night, is one way to support a person 'going out on the hill' seeking a vision. I recommend going with those that have gone before, and definitely in a group setting, where they can prepare you to be in the wilderness overnight. Perhaps there are two or three people wanting to go out on the hill and two or three that want to stay up all night feeding the fire. Then you can switch places at another time and return the favor.

In the back of the book, I have several suggestions for people who want a professional to help them with rites of passage.

Men's Groups-Forming Authentic Rites for Men

Robert Bly and other men, such as some male therapists, formed men's groups in the 80's and 90's that supported men in who they are, through poetry, and story. While these groups were somewhat controversial, due to sometimes supporting male domination over women, rather than breaking through conditioning to get to something more authentic, I feel they brought men to a new level of awareness around the question of what is a healthy and authentic man in the 21st century.

A group of men can form circles for themselves, however, to get past conditioning, it sometimes takes a leader with the awareness of guiding a group though the stereotypes to become more of who they are through encouraging self-expression, and releasing pent up feelings.

Since I am not a man, I have never attended one of these groups.

However, one such group I know of, use the same ritual components that I have described throughout the book; passing sage to smudge the room and each man in turn to set the tone; Creating a group intention supports the meeting purpose; passing a talking stick that the men create together, or some sort of object such as a stone, or bowl, or statue, helps everyone speak from the heart; concluding with song, or some sort of music, supports the theme of the night; and closing with releasing the directions, and having some food to share, basically sketches out the form of the evening.

For the right group of friends, you could do this on a fishing trip, on a camping trip, or just in your own backyard. It can be done after a game, or sporting event if the men are into sports and willing to share more deeply.

Some groups that I know of have been going for years, while others meet once a month, or once a quarter. Use your imagination, and if you want a terrific bonding experience, a heart centered ritual group can help.

11
Additional Adolescent Passages for Girls

Ritual Class for Girls
Mountain Art Center Adventure

Girl to Woman

Grasp a hand for help,
as she dies to toys and dolls,
while we form a mask of Earth,
and nurture her birth into womanhood.
She walks through the door of transition
to her new world emerging.

My class was filled with nine young girls from 9-14 at the Mountain Art Center in Ben Lomond, CA. The age spread of girls was a bit problematic. Some of them were clearly children, the older ones were budding women. But I felt that this group was self-selecting, and somehow they would bond. The class consisted of a week-long classes for 3 hours of poetry, mask making, art and costuming that would culminate in their transition from childhood to adulthood. Their parents were invited the last day, and we would create a rite that would acknowledge their transition together.

The Art Center Director and I had gotten a grant from the Santa Cruz Arts Foundation to pay my salary and cover supplies. We had been working on it for sometime before we began the class.

The first day all the girls and I sat around tables and after I explained the class to them, we talked about why they wanted to be in the class. They spoke about their fears of growing up and becoming a woman. To my surprise, they all had considerable fear of becoming a woman. While the girls were afraid of growing up, some were also excited by it. There was a lot more fear than joy. They were afraid of being hurt, raped, of not finding their place, their work, or their true love. They watched their mother's struggle and didn't like what they saw as far as the challenges each of their mother's faced.

So I read them some relevant poems, and then asked them to write a poem about their feelings. Then I asked them to go home at the end of the day, and interview their mothers and grandmothers about what they liked about being a woman for homework. The next day we would share their understanding and revelations. After we wrote poems, and shared them, I was startled at how well each child expressed their feelings. I was also startled at how diverse they were in their backgrounds, one child being Egyptian, one being Irish, one being African American, one being of mixed race, one Latina, one Jewish and so on. Each of them respected the other's background and family roots. It seemed we were learning from each other to form a new world together.

After the poems, writing and reading them, I asked them to paint a picture of their movement from childhood to adulthood. Some had images from their ancestry, some had bridges, or doors, and some had flying carpets to move through from one side to the other.

The next day after they had interviewed their mothers and grandmothers, we shared what they had learned from them. They realized that many of their mothers and grandmothers loved being a woman. They explained to some, that being a woman allowed them to love others and support the growth of their children and grandchildren. Some mothers had careers, some stayed at home. Many of their parents and grandparents enjoyed speaking to them about this important topic and the children grew closer to them as a result.

The second day, I noticed that the older children were forming a group, and there were some younger ones that were feeling left out. So I asked an older girl to become a partner to a younger one, for our next art project. We were going to make plaster masks.

These masks we would eventually paint. We would then create a costume about growing up from donated dresses from their families. I asked the mothers to bring old dresses and formals, and I stopped at a second-hand store to purchase some extras for the class.

Pairing the girls, older with a younger one, broke the clique's that were beginning to form, and helped to stop the 'them and us' mentality that is often prevalent with teenagers. It worked! Making masks can be a bit scary, so I wanted them to pair up for mutual support.

Each girl was to lay down on a table. Their helper or partner placed straws in their noses, and one in their mouth's to breathe with cotton and Vaseline as a sealer. A thin layer of Vaseline was spread over their faces, and was applied before the plaster bandages went on. Then they soaked plaster bandages in water, and applied wet plaster over their faces. This represented dying to their childhood, and being born to being a woman. I

68

explained this to them as each of the pairs worked together. They would be facing their fears of the unknown of becoming, just as they entered this initiation. I had extra pre-made plastic masks if they wanted to use them, but no one did!

We set up four tables with pillows and a cloth to catch the drips, and when they were comfortable, they greased their faces with Vaseline, and asked for help from their partners if they needed it. Then one would lay down on the table, and the other would talk them through the plaster as they dipped the bandages in water and laid them carefully around their faces, smoothing the edges and forming a mask. The girls could not move while the plaster was drying. To my surprise and delight, the girls each cared for each other so tenderly, no matter what age, and each of them came away with masks that they could decorate of their child face on the inside with their woman's face on the outside.

It was amazing to watch these girls go from childhood to adult-hood through the process of their creativity. When they were through, we set them out to dry to be painted the next day.

The third day, we met in a circle outside to talk about the masks and how we would paint them. I shared some meaningful tidbits around color, what they could mean connecting the girls to nature. So we imag-ined a color and associated it with nature. Green, grass, trees, bushes, etc. Red, flowers, blood, etc. Blue, sky, water, etc. I shared with them about the four directions, earth, air, water and fire, and how colors are associ-ated with the medicine wheel or the wheel of life; yellow for east, red for south, black for west, and white for north, with mother earth represented by green, and father sky, blue. The heart is often signified as purple, the center of the wheel.

Then I asked them about one thing that happened in their bodies that changed them forever from a child to a woman. Some of the older girls had started their bleeding. The younger girls knew about it, but had a lot of questions. I shared with them, that in a circle of women, it was usually okay to talk about being a woman and our bleeding time. I shared with them "moon time" from the Native people, and talked about other names that they had heard about that were not so wonderful. Then we spoke about what was really happening on their moon times and how each month they are releasing an egg and clearing off their uteruses for birth. Once they started their moon time, they could have a baby!

After our talk, they painted their masks. Some of the children used the colors symbolically, some of them painted what they felt about becom-ing a woman. They also made invitations to the rite of passage for their parents and grandparents.

The fourth day I brought a door on a frame that I got at a building recycling center. I set the door upright between two poles to stabilize it outside in the back yard of the art center. The door was painted white, and one side would be a painted with a group picture we created together about what it is to be a girl. The other side would be painted with what it was to be a woman. They would walk through this door on the last day to be presented to their parents. While the parents saw the group picture about being a girl, they would be walking through the door of womanhood, and as they stepped through it, the door swung open, and womanhood was presented along with each budding daughter.

On the last day, each of the girls got ready with their costumes and their masks. As they prepared, I greeted the parents and stood at the side of the door. When the parents were seated in front of the door, the girls each came up with their masks in a line. One by one, the girls stepped through it, then they stopped, I called their names, and sprinkled them with rose petals. After a girl was honored, they sat in a line in front to one side of the door until all of them had moved through the door. It was beautiful to watch these young women become women.

In the audience I noticed tears and deep reflections from their parents and grandparents. It was an important day, a day for them to move into their womanhood and be witnessed by their families. While this rite was offered as a class, it could be done with a group of mothers, or a group of women in a church setting, or in a neighborhood.

Raven's Rite

Raven had been thirteen, and was moving quickly into her teens. Her mother and I, who is my adopted daughter, decided we would do a ritual for her. The women and girls were asked to wear colors appropriate to their years, white for a small girl not yet menstruating, red for those menstruating, and purple for those past menopause.

When we lined up, we were quite a site, beginning with Raven, her mother and grandmother, then me, then from elders to youngsters, we processed out to the backyard to a place where we had laid blankets, and a chair with Raven's staff leaning against a tree.

Her dad had chosen her staff when she was born, and it was quite large with things we had tied on it to symbolize her strength and or dreams we had about her at her blessing way ceremony two weeks before she was born. Now we would add to her staff, tying red string with beads and other objects on it with a blessing for Raven as she entered her life as a budding young woman.

As we gathered in a circle on the blankets, (as I was leading the ritual) I passed the sage and lavender, and called in the four directions, Earth and Sky and Heart for the center. "We are here to honor Raven's rite of passage. Here is what we are going to do. First we will each tie on to her staff a red string with a bead, blessing, or whatever we choose. Then we will bless her with red rose petals. At the end we have a surprise! Is that okay with everyone?" Everyone nodded affirmatively.

Her mother began, with the story of her birth, and each of us in turn, shared our memories of that time and of what we knew about her from the beginning of her life. When we were through, the last woman whispered to Raven, "Raven, do you know what it means to be a menstruating woman? It means you can have a child of your own. It is a great responsibility, and a great blessing, both."

Then I took the roses, and asked each woman and girl to take three rose petals from their rose and bless Raven with her petals symbolizing the maiden, mother, and crone of womanhood, and then they were to give her the rest of the rose. After that, her mother gave her a crown of flowers, and new shoes that she wore back to the house. I opened the directions, and we had a feast afterwards. It was a memorable day for all of us.

Creating Your Own Rite for Womanhood

Traditionally in Africa and parts of Native America, a rite of passage would be offered by aunties for the daughters of their sisters. The reason for this is that it seems to be difficult to speak of sex and menses mother to daughter, as there is so much that may go on with family dynamics.

However you decide to create a rite to honor your daughters, all of these projects work well and build the momentum towards the culminating universal ceremony, ritual, or initiation. The rest is up to your imagination!

12
Honoring Who You Are as You Are

Ritual For gender Diverse People
Women Who Love Women Ritual

Kate and Mariah gathered us at their apartment. Kate had sent out an invitation on Facebook; "Come celebrate a night of 'Women who Love Women', whether you are a woman who loves women as a partner or as a sister…" the invitation went on…"This is a night to celebrate women."

When I entered their cozy apartment in Oakland, California, Kate had filled a large glass bowl with light blue water and lavender flowers and set it on the coffee table. We settled in around the table on chairs and a couch under the front picture window. Kate presented us each with a candle that she placed in front of us.

Four of us knew each other from Graduate school. One woman was a total stranger to me, and another was Mariah's friend. All were friend's of Kate's.

"So here we are," Kate began. "What I would like to do together is light the candle and say why we love women, and hold the lit candle. Then we'll go around again and say more if we want to and place the candle in the water. Does that sound okay to everyone?" We all nodded.

"Before we start I'd like to read a poem by Sappho to call in her spirit, the spirit of the goddess and bless out space. She read:

You are,
of all the unapproachable stars,
by far
the fairest,
the brightest—
possessing the Moon's splendor.22

Then Kate picked up a candle and Mariah handed her the lighter. As she lit the candle she said, "I have loved women for a long time. Some reasons I do are because women offer such comfort to each other. We can always find solace together."

Then I took the candle, setting an intention for a new book of po-

72

ems I was writing to honor the gentle wild, and saying that we need more gentleness in the world and that women bring this to men, women and children."

Each of us took our candle and lit it holding the lit votive in our hands and making statements about women, and how we loved what women bring to the world. On the second round, Kate added more of her feelings and placed her candle to float in the water. Then, remembering why I loved women, I added "I love women because when we need them they are here for us, and that makes such a difference." The rest of the women added their feelings and one by one we placed our candles to float together in blue water. Then Kate suggested we hold hands and said a thank you as we closed. I suggested a song that I had been given by Star Woman who is the 'Great Mother.' So we sang the song. which goes:

"One by one, the stars are lit, then we see the constellation,

One by one the stars are lit, then we see the beauty."

We sang it a few times. We could hear how the rounds were forming from the voices harmonizing together.

Afterwards we shared a pot-luck supper. What struck me about this circle was that it didn't matter to any of us if we were gay or straight. We came together to support each other in honoring women. Over dinner we discovered that of the six of us, three were straight, and three were gay. It was interesting to know, but it really didn't matter. We each loved women for what we brought to each other.

A Word about Feminine Initiation

While traditionally rites for women centered around menses and birth, today women have more choices then they did when I was growing up. Today women can be whatever they want to be, as well as mothers. For some of us motherhood passes us by, and we find ourselves adopting children, giving birth to projects or organizations, and supporting new opportunities for growth in other ways. My sense is that women need both rites that initiate the feminine—being—aspects of us, as well as the masculine—

doing—aspects as mentioned in the introduction. We all have a masculine and feminine aspect, however, if we don't honor both we become out of balance. The rites in this chapter are honoring menses, sexuality, and ways that we can move into the next parts of our lives in or out of relationships with men or other women.

13
Honoring Menses

Moon Hands

The moon's light rest
Lightly on my shoulders
She whispers to me proudly
and names me daughter.

Moon Time

I love the moon's fullness
I need her,
every month
she tells me woman's time.

Marsha, several other women, and I were sitting inside a large closet. The house Marsha lives in has the huge walk-in kind with windows inside that almost reach the floor. In one of the upstairs bedrooms, she cleaned out a closet that she rarely used anyway, and laid down some mats. She placed a large red rock inside with a slab of wood on top of it. Then she added candles and a little sage in a shell, creating an altar.

This is our moon lodge. Marsha put it together, and once a month she invites her friends to come over for rest, meditation, and to be in community with other women.

Sometimes we come alone when we are on our moon cycle to rest and meditate. Some of us have added flowers and favorite stones, metals, and pendants. Because we are from a variety of religious traditions, the altar in the moon lodge was not focused strictly on one spiritual tradition, but honors all religions and races. For many of us it has become a sanctuary from our hectic lives.

During our gathering this particular month, we found ourselves rubbing each other's feet and talking about our families, our pasts, our careers, and problems we were having. Some of us shared what we found to be useful self-help tools. Sometimes we spread the tarot; other times we meditated together, or prayed, or drummed. For some of us it was a new experience to be supported and nourished by other women. Our time together was important in healing past injuries.

Affirming one another's decisions and supporting each other's growth seemed to be the most important aspect of the moon lodges, especially when it came to talking about our bodies and our monthly cycles. Through the years of meeting together, we have learned a great deal from each other and from various teachers.

We first met as a group in a class on Native American spirituality. Over the years we continue to meet, gathering with our families for classes or a picnics, but the discussions among the women always seems to turn, at some point, to our struggles with our changing views of ourselves. We recognize the bond we share with all women through our monthly cycle, and with all of the women through time. We have spent many hours learning about the traditional Native American views that honor women's monthly flow. We support each other in our spiritual practice, which includes regarding our bodies as sacred, especially during menses.

We adopted the Native American way of speaking of our periods as our "moontime." When we are menstruating we are on our moon. This seems to all of us a much more positive and life-affirming way to address menstruation. Every month, when we feel our menses about to start, we try to take some time to rest and be alone. Sometimes we even take the day off from work, if we can afford it. Our monthly flow is a natural purification process, and our bodies need time to rest and restore themselves.

As women we are an extension of the earth itself. Our bodies reflect the earth's sacred receptive nature. Offering the first monthly blood flow to the Mother is a way to honor that connection and surrender to our bodily process.

In my own monthly practice, I sometimes buried or burned the first tampon. Sometimes I have planted a little blood on a tissue in a designated place in the garden, then watered it, returning it to the Mother. Sometimes, if I am alone, I go outside at night and squat on the earth, offering the blood directly.

During the full moon I sometimes spend time taking a moon bath. Many of my friends and I find ourselves enjoying solitary walks at night—in safe places—during the full moon. We often gather on the full moon, share our problems, and set our intention for personal change in the coming month. Sometimes we walk together, enjoying the full moon's light. I feel as if the energy from the moon is feeding me.

Inside my house I have created an altar, which changes during my moon time. I rearrange things, or put a new scarf under the objects. A round red box sits in the center, and I close it during the days of my moon. I may retrieve pictures of women saints or goddesses I admire.

On my body I wear different earrings designated for my moon time. Sometimes I wear them for a day, sometimes longer. Often I wear red or orange, and I sometimes take special baths with rose petals floating in the water.

The blood we lose is releasing and cleansing our bodies. Even if a woman is no longer shedding blood, either through hysterectomy or menopause, these monthly rites could still be considered a way to take time out, rest, and restore oneself.

Creating Rites of Menses

Using our monthly cycle to rest has been a practice in many indigenous cultures for centuries. Secret rites of womanhood, which included initiating women into their roles and responsibilities as mothers, wives, and food gatherers, as well as into sacred knowledge of the body, was the primary purpose of these rites. Today we have nearly lost connection with the sacred through our bodies. Reframing the negative messages into positive ones takes vigilant observation of what we tell ourselves as well as societal messages we accept as true.

Creating monthly rites, however simple, help us remember how beautiful and sacred a vessel our bodies are, which is the primary purpose for doing those rites. When several women meet on a monthly basis, you can create support group that helps everyone. If you have daughters, give them support and blessing during their monthly flow. It helps them grow up with a better self-image.

Here are some suggestions:

* Schedule time for yourself during the full moon or during the first day(s) of your monthly cycle.

* Take a private area of the house, or top of a dresser, bookcase, or shelf of a closet and create an altar there. Let your family know it is a place for you and no one else, unless you choose to share it. Set important things on it that are just for you and use it as a place of focus for prayer and meditation. It can also be a room for exploring creative ideas, like an artist's studio. Let yourself create pictures or poems, or keep a journal or write or sing songs there.

* Make a commitment to yourself to take time out.

* For a moon time support group, talk to other women about this chapter. You don't need many women, three or four will do. Here are more suggestions:

* Make a commitment to meet every month.

* Pass the leadership from person to person so no one feels over-burdened. (You can also make it a leaderless group.)

* The leader of the month can bring something specific to share, or can choose an activity or a topic for discussion. Here are some suggestions:

* Drum together—drums are the heartbeat of the earth and can transform your mood and temperament.

* Create rites together to transform and heal each other during difficult times.

* Give each other shoulder massages—it's a great way to bond, and helps one another relax.

* Pass around a talking stick, and use the group to tell the truth of how you really feel in that moment. If you have time limits, use a timer.

* Brainstorm together about what each of you want from the group.

* Create rites of passage for yourself or your daughters that will positively affirm womanhood.

* Dream together of how different our planet would be if every group of women had their own moon circle honored.

14
A Womanhood Celebration

Redwood Wedding

A rock shaped like a heart
inside a tree?

I curl into it
and sit in the deep drone
it makes, regarding its curves
and resident spiders.
I am at home here.

Others come blowing by
but do not change
the music inside the tree.
A child cries in the distance.
Flute notes drift up from the valley.
Rusty bark catches the light.

There is a wedding going on inside.

Four trusting souls were following me into the redwoods at sunset. I hoped we could find our way out when the evening was over. For a moment I nervously wondered how I got into the position I was in—leading a ceremony for my friend Karen, assuming that together we would pull it all together without a dry run. I kept calm by remembering all the other rituals I had created. I knew I could do it and, at the same time, I was really feeling the weight of responsibility.

Karen's confidence in me helped. We had developed the event largely in tandem; I knew I wasn't solely responsible for its success. Everything would work out as it was supposed to be. After all, she trusted me enough to let me choose the site.

I knew the perfect spot. I led them to a lovely green field surrounded by a deep forest. But when we arrived, we were surprised to find an energetic group of Boy Scouts playing games. I tried not to let this shake my confidence. We wandered farther down a trail until we could no longer hear the voices of the boys. It was getting so dark we finally picked a wide, level, clear spot on the trail and declared it 'the place.'

As we looked up, we could see the silhouettes of the trees making a ring around us. We were protected by a hill that rose from the opposite side of the trail. There was no poison oak, at least as far as we could see in the encroaching darkness. I began to relax a little, breathing in the scent of eucalyptus mixed with the cool night air. We spread our blankets. Karen laid out some of the items she had brought, and we took our places in a circle.

In our conversations prior to gathering that evening, Karen spoke of the impact of turning thirty. She knew her thirties were about something different than her twenties had been. She wanted to be conscious of the qualities within herself that she was ready to release, and which ones she wanted to embrace. I had asked Karen to think about them and make two lists in preparation. I suggested she ask herself what it meant to her to be a woman, and how she was becoming more of herself as a result of making this transition. I asked her to look at her faith, what elements had meaning for her, and which ones had lost their significance.

Although Catholic by birth, Karen had found more meaning in religions centered around nature. We decided to use several selections from a book of rituals by Starhawk called The Spiral Dance. Karen had asked each of us to share a poem or give a statement that would help give her the encouragement she needed to enter the next phase of her life. She also thought about the friends she wanted to support her and witness her transition into womanhood. She chose her boyfriend, Jake; a friend, Darlene; and an older friend, Gladys.

I developed a program from our conversations and brought it along for each participant. The sheet helped everyone follow the sequence of events and provided Karen with a memento.

Once we were seated comfortably, Jake began by honoring the four directions. In earth-based spiritual traditions, the four directions represent not only north, east, south, and west, but aspects of ourselves that are reflected in nature, such as power, creativity, vulnerability, and growth. They also symbolize the four elements—earth, air, fire, and water—the four seasons, the four races of humanity, and so on. (See Chapter 2, "Creating Ceremonies from the Heart.") Jake asked the spirit of those qualities, represented in each direction and within each of us, to be with us to support Karen.

Then I read "The Charge of the Goddess" from Starhawk's book. It poetically speaks of our connection with the earth and our integral relationship with her through the mystery within us, that to know ourselves is to know the universe in all its wonder.

Then Darlene read a poem by the thirteenth-century Persian mystic Rumi called "Give Yourself a Kiss." The translation was from Colman Barks's book of Rumi's poetry called *Like This*, and it reinforced the words from "The Charge of the Goddess." Darlene had not told Karen what she was going to read. We were surprised by how the two passages complimented one another so perfectly.

> Give yourself a kiss.
> If you live in China,
> > don't look somewhere
> > else, in Tibet or Mongolia.
>
> If you want to hold the beautiful
> > one,
> > hold yourself to yourself.
>
> When you kiss the Beloved,
> > touch your own lips with your
> > > own fingers.
>
> The beauty of every woman and every
> > man is your own beauty.
>
> The confusion of your hair
> > obscures that sometimes.
> An artist comes to paint you
> > and stands with his mouth open.
>
> Your love reveals your beauty,
> > but all coverings would
> > disappear if only for a moment
> > your holding-back would sit
> > before your generosity and ask,
> > > "Who are you?"
> > > At that,
> The Beloved's life-changing face
> > gives you a wink.

We sat in silence for a moment after each reading. The night wind picked up slightly, and we listened to the branches of the trees rustle above us.

Then Jake lit the Epsom salts and rubbing alcohol in the small iron pot Karen had brought. The two chemicals made a cool flame in the center of the circle, representing the center of the universe, the center of love in each soul. Karen had meditated on her inner male and wrote what came to her. Jake read:

Part of becoming a woman is the full integration of her male energy with her female energy. Honoring the inner male is to celebrate the qualities within her that will keep her wild and sexual, strong and swift, powerful and passionate. The inner male in her will never be fully tamed or domesticated. Through this male energy, she will know the essence of manifestation—she will know the undivided self.

Karen read slowly the qualities of which she was letting go, and put them one by one into the kettle. Her list read:

impatience
impetuousness
judgment
fear of not being heard or seen
procrastination
irresponsibility
trying to be what I think others want me to be
jumping to conclusions
lack of decorum
restlessness
the internal cynic
vanity

In the dimly lit flames, I could see her face change as each one dissipated within her. Even though the qualities may show themselves again, she was consciously choosing not to give them power over her any longer. As she burned the paper in the kettle, the fire went out and we lit our flashlights.

Then Karen asked Gladys to move next to her for the blessing portion of the ritual. Gladys is Karen's surrogate grandmother. She was always available to Karen when Karen needed to talk. Gladys also helped her by freely sharing her own experiences with Karen when asked. Their relationship was a very special one and the love they shared seemed to glow that evening.

Gladys took a little of the water and sprinkled it on Karen's head, face, arms, and hands with each of the qualities she wanted to cultivate:

inquisitiveness

playfulness

wonder

openness to possibilities

awe of nature

spontaneity

psychic gifts

energy

desire

passion

creativity

ability to think on my feet

courage

sense of humor

joy

Karen received each drop of water as blessing her body, mind, and spirit. I was very honored to be in the presence of such love. It was clear to me that Gladys was receiving as much from giving to Karen, as Karen was receiving from a truly wise elder.

Then it was my turn. I had prepared a guided inner journey for Karen. I asked that everyone close their eyes and benefit in their own way.

Take a few deep breaths, allowing each breath to take you deeper and deeper into yourself. On the fourth breath, focus your attention on your heart center. Within your heart center is a beautiful green field. Smell the wildflowers and the freshness of the grasses. On the edge of the field is a deep forest with a trail that beckons you. Allow yourself to follow the path, which was meant for you. Feel the coolness of the woods and the subtle colors of the shadows. At the end of the trail is the mouth of a cave. This is your secret cave; no one else can enter it without your permission. It may appear to be an earthen cave, or one made of crystal; whatever its configuration, it is for you and you alone. You are drawn inside. You find several steps and enough light to see your way down them. There may be a torch, or the walls may be lit from within and glow; however you choose to light your path, let this be your design. Descending the stairs, you see a light at the bottom. A room opens and a place is made for you. There is a bath waiting, and robes. Enter the bath and allow the water to clean away any distracting thoughts or tensions. When you feel fully relaxed, notice the beautiful robes. Feel their texture and the perfume that may be present in the air. Allow yourself to experience this space in whatever way holds meaning for you.

Now you notice another entrance to a stairway that goes even deeper into the earth. You are drawn to the edge of it and notice a torch or light for you inside the door. Enter through the door and descend the stairs. You begin to hear drumbeats in the distance coming from the bottom of the stairwell. Notice what the stairs are made of. Are they stone or earth? You descend for a long time until you reach the bottom. The drumbeats are louder now and steady, and you move in the direction of the sound. You reach the chamber of the Wise Ones.

Here are assembled those who will teach you and guide you on your way. They have a space for you to sit and join them. Join the circle now. Greet each one as you go around the circle. Look into their faces and recognize each one as you acknowledge their place in this important council. Notice what they wear, how they sit. Feel the blessing of this group. You have come for the first time. They welcome you. They present you with a gift. Is it in a box or wrapping? Allow yourself to receive it and open it now. What is this gift? Now you have a gift for them. What is it? Ask for what you need to know at this time; perhaps you have come with a question. Hear the answer, feel the truth of it.

It is time to say good-bye to the council. Know that you can return whenever and as often as you like. Your council may change, depending on your needs; just remember that anyone you ask to be there will be present. Now ask the council if there is anything else you need to know at this time. Receive it and thank them for these gifts. Allow yourself to acknowledge their wisdom with a bow or a touch of your hand—whatever feels appropriate. Take you leave, and say good-bye.

Find your way back to the edge of the stairs with the light you carry. Walk up the flight of stairs to the top. Now you are in the first room you came to. Stay in this room for a little while, if you wish, and when you are ready, walk slowly up the stairs to the entrance of the cave. Now you are at the top of the cave. Take a deep breath, smelling the freshness of the air and the beauty of the forest. Follow the path through the woods and, when you are ready, enter the field and enjoy the brightness of the day. Take another deep breath, remembering all that you learned, carrying with you the gifts you received. When you are ready, slowly bring yourself back to the redwoods, outside of Oakland, California. Tune in to the sounds of the night all around us, wiggle your toes, stretch, and open your eyes.

Everyone began to move around, shaking out limbs and stretching. By the expressions on their faces, I noticed that everyone, including

Karen, had received something important from their inner council.

When we were ready, Karen reached for a pot of soil that she brought, along with seeds she intended to plant, for the next part of her rite. She said, "Now I will evoke to qualities of womanhood I want to cultivate in my life." She took a seed for each quality and slowly planted:

patience
decorum
compassion
commitment
a sense of time and timing
gentleness
perspective
listening skills
meditation
discernment
humility
productivity
discipline
inner beauty

I could feel each seed being internalized by Karen in a most beautiful and loving way.

Then Gladys spoke. She gave each of us a copy of what she was about say:

I am here to give the view from the mountain, the Crone's view. To share with you Karen, what wisdom I have gained through living out a good part of the full circle of cycles of this one lifetime. I have known the spring, the summer, the fall, and now I am beginning the winter season. All have had their special gifts and difficult learning. Yes, here I am almost sixty-five, a benchmark year and what do I know?

I know that I am part of Forever
and I know that I have just begun.

Now, with that background let's turn to the task at hand.

I reach out for you with all that I am. I reach out and welcome you into selfhood as a woman.

I celebrate what is and what has been happening. I celebrate your coming into yourself.

I look at you, Karen, and what do I find? I find great beauty. I look at you, Karen, and what do I find?

84

An honesty that I greatly admire. In my own life when I can let in the 'is-ness,' when I don't have to turn from honest hate, anger, disgust, fear, or pain but can live it out of me, then I know the wings of joy.

When in your journey you find you need comforting, if it would help to be held, to be rocked, to be told you are loved,

I am available.

When in your journey you need to share your accomplishments, celebrate your creations, or need a listener as you give voice to new insights,

I am available.

Welcome, dear Karen, to it all, to the pain and the joy and to the challenge of being the new woman,

for the new age
that has just begun.
I love you.

Gladys.

Needless to say there was not a dry eye in the woods that night. Karen deeply felt the blessing from Gladys.

As the ritual was drawing to a close, Jake spontaneously suggested that we sing a song to Karen. We sang the "River is Flowing," which begins:

The river is flowing, flowing and growing,
the river is flowing down to the sea.
Mother carry me, a child I will always be,
Mother carry me, down to the sea.

To close, we joined hands and recited a prayer from Starhawk's The Spiral Dance:

From the Earth that is her body, to the Air that is her breath, to the Fire of her bright spirit, to the Waters of her living womb, may the peace of the Goddess always be in your heart, merry meet, merry part and merry meet again. The circle is open but unbroken. Blessed be.

Before gathering our things, I surprised Karen with a necklace that had belonged to me. She was delighted as she had secretly wanted some jewelry to commemorate the event. After exchanging hugs, we gathered our things and slowly found our way out of the woods and back to the car. We walked quietly, feeling the blessing of the evening and noticing the stars shining brightly overhead. I felt so grateful for being a part of such a loving event. All the anxiety I experienced going into the ritual had vanished. Everything unfolded exactly as it was meant to be.

We ended the evening with a small party for the five of us at Gladys's house. The warmth between us spread throughout the evening as we shared cookies, cake, and tea. I drove home feeling happy and peaceful.

Creating Your Own Ritual of Womanhood

Not everyone is involved in earth-based spiritual traditions and would produce a ritual of this kind. However, the basic components could be adapted to suit other religious traditions. The basic format—letting go of the past, affirming the future, and reflecting on personal growth—could serve anyone contemplating this kind of ceremony.

To begin, ask yourself some basic questions:

* What are the qualities that you want to release from the past?

* What are the new qualities that you want to express or continue into the rest of your life?

* What does it mean for you to be a woman, or of your gender preference?

* Are the qualities you have chosen, helping you become more yourself?

* Whom would you like to help you celebrate your transition?

* What objects would you like to use that have meaning for you? This could be jewelry, hair ornaments, pieces of cloth, or something from your mother or grandmothers, fathers or brothers.

* What elements (earth, air fire, and water) are appropriate to include in this rite?

* Where would you hold such an event?

* How would you like to open the ritual?

* What would you declare and embrace as the center of the ritual?

* How would you close?

15

Self-Discovery Ceremony

Feather and Claw

The heron has always been here.
But it's you I cannot see.
Scratching and biting me
in the dark,
the wild thing that you are,
Please give me no rest,
don't let me
fall back to sleep.

"Do it!" she said emphatically. "You will never regret it, and if you don't try, you will always wonder what it would have been like." Coco had leaned over the table where we were sitting, less than a foot away from my face. She was a woman I had known less than an hour, yet in that moment she was my best friend. There was no escaping her words. I knew she was right and if I didn't try, even though I was petrified with fear, I would always regret it.

Her face was softly wrinkled and kind. She was an elder, shocking me into following the path before me, like a voice from God saying: "Make no mistake, this is your life, do with it what you will." She was daring me to move from visual art to performance art, which was a giant step. If I performed the work I had in mind, I would expose the core of my character, flaws and all. What's more, I would have to stand more fully in my power as a creative woman. There was no more compromising myself. This would challenge my relationship with my husband, which was already difficult enough.

In the brief hour we spent together, Coco shared the photos of the performance pieces she had done in New York. Listening to her descriptions, I was struck by how similar the unfolding process of her work was to my own. After sharing with her the similarity of our experiences, I could not escape her challenge, yet I had no idea how I would find the courage to present the piece in the small, insular community in which I lived.

I had met Coco and her companion, George, through Ted. Ted and I were mounting a national handmade-paper exhibit, opening that night in Ann Arbor, Michigan. Ted was the curator, and I was assisting him in hanging the second in a series of traveling shows, which we had organized together. We both had original artwork in the exhibit, along with many other artists from across the country. I was thrilled to meet other artists using the same media. Coco was from New York, George from Canada. The two of them had driven together for the opening. Meeting George and Coco was a wonderful experience. It seemed an extra bonus that Coco was also a performance artist, inspiring me in two media.

I had been studying Coco since she got out of the beat-up station wagon they had arrived in. She was a remarkably free spirit. I liked her wildness, perhaps secretly wanting to express more of it in my own life.

Doing this performance ritual was just what I needed to do to support my creative and feminine blossoming. It would provide me with the physical experience to embody change. My artwork had always provided me a way to look at my inner process. It was a terrific form of therapy. Naturally, the transition I was beginning showed up first in the art I was producing. My work began to flow from visual art to performance art, the natural next step, but it was a terrifying one because working in the studio alone was so private, and now I would be performing in front of other people.

As serendipity would have it, after the opening in Ann Arbor, I was scheduled to attend a Jackson Area Dance Council board meeting the very next week. We were planning the annual May dance performance. At the end of the meeting, I nervously announced my request to perform the piece I called "Feather and Claw." My request was greeted enthusiastically. I asked for assistance from two dancers on the council who were friends of mine. They were very happy to be a part of it. We set a date for the performance.

The deadline forced me to commit to working on the piece. I had never given any kind of public performance in my life, except for nightmarish piano recitals as a child. Needless to say, I was terrified.

Three factors helped me belayed my anxiety. The first was that the Dance Council was full of very dear, supportive people whom I had known personally and professionally for several years. Another was that I had a nagging feeling that I had to publicly perform the work. I had no idea why; in fact it made no logical sense at all to me. But my body knew. It was important to dance the piece, to embody the change. Intuitively I also knew that it was important to create the work in front of an audience. The audience became an important part of the work as I soon discovered. The third factor was Coco's timely challenge; without it, I would not have considered performing at all.

Months before I had met Coco, the idea for "Feather and Claw" had begun. It developed from some reading I had done on native Hawaiian spirituality. One book by Serge King called Kahuna Healing described three levels of a person: the higher self, the middle self, and the lower self. The lower self represented our animal nature, which some Hawaiian people relate to actual animals. Through the meditation exercises in the book, one could discover the animal of the lower self.

I was fascinated with the idea and set out to discover my animal nature. I already knew that part of my higher nature was birdlike; I related to the Great Blue Heron. Yet I felt there was another animal I wasn't recognizing as part of my lower self.

After weeks of practicing the meditations and trying the exercises unsuccessfully, I decided to speak with my friend Jane about my experiences. I shared the book and my frustrations using the meditations. I felt blocked and asked her if she saw something in me I couldn't see.

She knew me well. As I spoke I could see a wide, loving grin spread across her face. She said, "Robin, it is so obvious; you're a cat." Immediately I pushed away her suggestion. I hated cats. They were so sneaky and independent—so many characteristics I didn't admire. How could I be a cat?! I could see that Jane had no stake at all in being right about the cat theory. She was simply stating the obvious. I told her I'd think about it. She just smiled.

By the time we met again, I had done a lot of thinking about myself as a cat. The idea was still uncomfortable to me, but I knew she was right. Through Jane's honesty and my willingness to take a hard look at myself, I learned there were parts of myself I didn't like. To reconcile these conflicting aspects, I toyed with the bird and the cat inside myself and watched their interactions. I also took long walks in nature and laid on the earth. It was through this process that the ritual dance was created.

After my dinner with Coco, I spent the next few months preparing for the ritual. I designed costumes with Lisa, a friend, colleague, and excellent seamstress. I made bird and cat masks out of basket materials, and Lisa sewed the costumes which slipped over leotards that the dancers wore. Music was selected by me with the help of my husband, Jason, who played the songs on his guitar. I was hoping his involvement would help bring us closer together. As it turned out it was too little too late; however, the process of making costumes and selecting music helped me integrate the two animals within myself.

Over the months of preparation, I had spoken to the two dancers,

Julie and Monette, about what I was discovering about myself internally. A few weeks before the performance the three of us met. I gave them their costumes and discussed with them the specific animals they were to represent. Both dancers were so enthusiastic they took time with living birds and cats, observing and copying their movements. Because the dancing was to be largely improvisational, they each choose to embody as much animal movement as possible before the performance. I was delighted by their energy and dedication to the dance we were about to create together.

The day of the performance arrived. "Feather and Claw" was the last piece on the Dance Council's spring program. My nervousness had not subsided, but I was willing to go ahead. After my piece was announced, I asked the audience to sit in a large circle on the floor of the theater.

I began the piece by escorting the two dancers into the center of the circle, where I dressed them in their costumes. The act of dressing them was a way for me to symbolically accept responsibility for creating the animal images within myself. One dancer was the bird, dressed in blue; the other was the cat, dressed in dark red. I represented the observer within and wore a blue leotard and a skirt of both red and blue.

Next I spread white butcher paper around the edge of the circle at the feet of the audience. We made tucks in the paper to conform to the circle. The cat, the bird, and I each sprinkled colored tempera around the circle on the paper. The paper and the colors were a way to mark a sacred space in which to move. The audience, who sat around us on the floor, were there as witnesses. Symbolically, I was separating myself from the outer world in order to do my inner work. It was also a way for me to acknowledge the transition from two-dimensional art to performance art.

The music began and I danced with the bird first while the cat was silent. When the cat began to dance, she cautiously tapped my shoulder, which I ignored. Gradually she resorted to more drastic measures until she finally "clawed" my back and I was forced to turn and recognize her.

As I kept pushing her away, the cat began to toy with me until I played with her, and the two of us began to move together. Slowly as I made peace with cat, the bird began to dance. I left their company to watch the two interact. The dance roughly followed my inner process, this time with the audience witnessing.

The bird and the cat fought, moving around each other with great caution and disgust. Slowly they began to find a way to move together. When they were comfortably dancing in a new, more harmonious rhythm, I rejoined them, and the three of us completed the dance. At the end of the performance, I opened the circle of painted paper and we paraded around the audience, encouraging them to join us in the dance.

Through performing the work I realized how vital it was to have an audience. It was a new experience to feel community support for my inner process. People I knew and loved became my tribe. I was the initiate. They were able to help me validate my need for inner work and reintegrate into the community, as so many tribal initiates have done before me. My friend Jane had been the Wise One whom I conferred with over inner matters. She had acted like the tribal teacher who councils the younger members before initiation. Coco was an elder too, but in the form of the trickster who shocked me into going ahead with performing the work.

A few years later I would learn that "Feather and Claw" followed tribal initiations very closely. It corresponded to Arnold Van Gennep's observations of rites that included three distinct parts: separation, transition, and incorporation. It reinforced my understanding that within our intuition lie the patterns we need to create rituals. Each of us has our own expression of it.

The dance was presented twice at two important junctures in my life. The first was the May Dance Council performance. It marked a time when it became increasingly obvious to me that as I grew in self-awareness, I seemed to alienate my husband. It was actually the beginning of the end of our relationship. I was beginning a more primary and essential relationship within myself.

The second performance took place a year later at the museum where I had worked as a curator for five and a half years. It was presented by the Dance Council at a young people's art fair. The second performance gave me an opportunity to bring closure to my career. In the time between performances I had gone through a divorce and resigned from the museum.

Both performances were a way for me to acknowledge myself in front of and in honor of the people and places that helped me grow. It was a way for me to respectfully decline further participation with them and to honor my inner process, which was leading me in new directions. In my own divine drama, I was acting out the closing phase of my life as I had known it, to begin new adventures on my own.

Inspiring Your Own Ritual of Self-Affirmation

I share this ritual with you to inspire confidence. It takes a certain craziness to perform a ritual among people that have known you in one way, and expose your inner conflicts to them, perhaps giving them a different, more honest view of yourself. Perhaps you are not an artist living in a mostly blue-collar town, as I was in Jackson; but if I can do a performance ritual there, you can do yours anywhere, in your own way and in your own community. Just allow your childlike nature to play with the inner images of who you are. It will produce the most amazing results!

To get you started, try this meditation; have ready three large pieces of paper, crayons or markers, and a candle:

1. Light a candle and sit quietly in front of it. Close your eyes and take a few deep, slow breaths. Let yourself go inside. On the winds of your breathing, imagine a feather drifting from the top of your head, through your body, to the base of your spine. Imagine you are seeing an animal running free and wild in your belly. What animal is it?

2. Now imagine that you have a bird circling overhead. What kind is it?

3. Let the two animals live freely inside you. How do they interact?

4. Without disturbing your inner discovery, take three separate pieces of paper and draw each of the animals and then their combined interaction.

5. Next look into your heart and see a garden there. Let the animals come together inside your heart-garden. Imagine a very wise and loving being there, helping the two animals know each other better. When you are ready, take three more deep breaths and slowly come back into the room. You can return anytime to these three locations inside you—just follow the previous steps.

To further explore these animals and their movements, ask yourself: "What are their movements?" Dance out the movements of each animal, allowing yourself the freedom to move as they would move. Write about your experiences. Use the encyclopedia or library resources to understand more about your animals.

As you work with them over time, your animals may change, depending on where you live and your experiences in life. The bird generally represents your higher self or wisdom nature. The other animal represents your creative and sexual energy. Studying them both can give you clues about your own nature, increasing self-awareness and self-acceptance.

It may be more natural for you to draw, sing, drum, write, chant, hum, or laugh your way into more of yourself. However you access your creativity is wonderful and unique for you.

How would you develop your own ritual of self-affirmation from the two animals you have discovered within yourself? If you tell the story of your self-discovery in movement, pictures, poetry or prose, or any combination, you can begin to form your rite. Stories and rites usually have a beginning, a middle, and an end. You have already begun your ritual by separating yourself from others and going within. The next step is transition, which is expressed by drawing them or making the images. Incorporation takes place by embodying these animals through movement.

Next ask yourself what elements (earth, air, fire, and water) you arc drawn to. Perhaps you have a small group of friends who are willing to share their stories, too. Take turns enacting you self-discovery rites.

Combined with the rituals in chapters 17 and 18, the following three stories show how I assisted myself through the process of changing my life. I offer them to you in hopes that they may provide inspiration and suggestions in your evolving story.

16
Miscarriage

For a Moment . . .

You were here
like a new revolving planet.
But something knocked you
off course.
Something has thrown you
out of the sky.

Jane felt fine until the bleeding started. She had been pregnant less than eight weeks when she began to feel sharp pains in her abdomen. She called the doctor immediately. Then she called her husband, Rick. He came home from work to take her to the doctor. In the car they expressed their fears and nervousness. This was their first baby, and they weren't sure what was happening.

At the doctor's office they found out. Jane might be miscarrying. The doctor told her to go home and rest, take off the next few days from work. If the bleeding gets worse, she may have to go to the hospital. By afternoon she felt the cramping increase. By that night she had miscarried.

The bleeding under control, she felt better physically, but was so depressed she could not stop crying. Rick decided to call her parents to let them know what had happened.

"Let me talk to her, Rick," Jane's mother, Marge, said firmly. Rick handed the phone to Jane.

"Mom?" Jane burst into tears.

"It's all right, honey. You just go ahead and cry." After Jane wept for several minutes, Marge said, "Jane, I never told you this, but before you were born I miscarried, too. It was really hard at the time. But I know you will get through this."

Her mother talked more openly than she had ever spoken to her before. Jane felt her mother's reassurance, and really appreciated her first-hand experience. Jane loved feeling her mother's support. It calmed her and helped her realize she wasn't alone.

"What are you doing this weekend?" her mother asked. "Your dad and I want to come visit. Is that okay with you?" Jane spoke to Rick and they agreed.

The next morning Jane felt well enough to call a few close friends and tell them what had happened. She also shared her mother's positive response to her trauma. Two friends asked to meet Marge when she came for the visit.

When Saturday came, Marge, Char, Pam, and Jane were sitting around the table. Her friends brought Jane a large bunch of balloons to cheer her up. Rick and Ed, Jane's father, had just left for a football game. As the four women shared tea, Jane told Marge how much it meant to her to have her support.

"Mom, Pam and Char wanted to meet you. I am so grateful that you were really there for me."

Marge reached over and took Jane's hand. "How are you doing now, honey?"

Jane looked down into her hands. "I feel really sad, and full of guilt, like there is something wrong with me."

Marge sat back in her chair, raised an eyebrow, and stated firmly, "Jane, there is no shame in miscarrying—it is quite common. The Creator is just getting you ready for the next time. You know, you are not the only one to go through this. Your dad's sister Betty and Aunt Rene and I have all miscarried. I know you really wanted this child, but sometimes if things aren't right, it's for the best."

Pam added, "When my sister Sheila miscarried, we did a little ritual that helped her release some of her feelings. Why don't the four of us do something today, while the men are gone. We've got all afternoon."

Marge looked a little skeptical. "What do you mean by 'ritual,' Pam?"

"It's a way for us to be with Jane as she moves through her feelings. We will be creating time for her to grieve, to let go, and move on," Pam explained.

"I like the idea," said Jane. "Tell me about your sister's ritual."

Pam drew her chair closer to the table.

"Well, we sat in a circle. Sheila sat to the south, which can represent death, birth, and the connection to the spirit world, according to a Native American friend who helped us with it. The north represents power, east is new beginning, and west is water, flow, change, and sometimes death. Sheila spoke of her loss and of her sorrow. As she stated each feeling, the rest of us repeated Sheila's words back to her. It sounded a little like an echo, but it was very helpful for Sheila to hear her feelings affirmed. Then she spoke to a doll wrapped in a blanket, as though it were the lost child, and told it all her regrets and sorrow about the loss. As she cried and expressed her feelings, she began to affirm her desire for the future, too, when the child could come through her. Then each woman shared insights and feelings from her own experience, and the ritual was over."

Marge crossed her arms. "I don't know about this doll business. It sounds a little weird to me. You girls go ahead."

Jane took her mother's hand. "Mom, we don't have to do it that way. Please share this with me."

Marge looked at Jane for a moment. She thought about her daughter's loss and how grateful she was to have Jane in her life. She could not deny her daughter's sincere request.

"Okay, honey," Marge relented. "You tell me what it is you want me to do and I'll do it with you."

Then Char spoke up. "Listen, everybody. We could use the balloons and release them one at a time for each of Jane's feelings! Some for regrets and some for blessings. We could go into the backyard or down by the park or something."

"Now that's an idea that sounds good to me," agreed Marge.

"Me, too!" Jane said.

Pam nodded in agreement. "I like it."

Jane added, "I don't feel ready to see anyone else. Let's use the backyard—I love our big oak tree."

The four women walked through the living room toward the backyard.

"I need to see the balloons pop," said Jane. "Somehow that's important. I want to pop them myself. I'll use Aunt Betty's old hat pin. That way, Dad's side of the family will have a symbolic presence. I'll meet you outside." She smiled as she thought of her father's sister Betty, and left the group to retrieve the pin.

When she returned, they gathered in a circle under the oak tree. Jane held the balloons.

Pam began, "Let's take three deep breaths together to help us begin." Then Pam looked at her friend Jane; she noticed how much more calm she seemed now than when Pam had first arrived.

"I'm so glad you're all here with me. I feel so much better than I did on Tuesday. Thank you for being with me today, sharing this important time with me." She looked at each one as she spoke.

Then she took a balloon from the bunch and said slowly, "I feel so

96

sad that I'm not pregnant." Jane's voice cracked. As she wept, the women paused to let her cry. Then they repeated her statement. When they had finished, Jane popped the balloon.

She took another balloon and said, "I feel bad that I couldn't prevent this miscarriage." Again the women repeated her feelings and Jane popped the balloon. When she had gone through several balloons, she noticed her mother's tears. "Mom, are you okay?"

"I was just remembering that baby I never had, this brings it all back." At that, Jane handed her mother some balloons, and Marge released a few to acknowledge her own feelings and the loss she had never grieved. The women echoed each of her statements.

Then Char spoke up. "Jane, can I pop a balloon? I want to bless my nephew who died as an infant." When she was finished, Pam shared her sadness over the loss of her sister Sheila's unborn child. As the women cried and the balloons burst, each woman shared the losses she had experienced.

For the last several balloons, the four women held the strings together and popped them in turn. The last few blessed the spirit of the child.

At the last balloon, Jane said, "I love you and bless you, little spirit. I hope you will try again when it's the right time."

Then she released the balloon into the tree. A gust of wind guided the balloon away from the sharp branches. The string on the balloon was caught for a moment, but then another gust took the balloon high into the sky. The women watched it for as long as they could see it.

When the last balloon had disappeared, the ritual seemed over in a natural way. The four women stood together with their arms around each other. They swayed in silence for a long time, listening to the wind rustle in the branches overhead.

Creating Your Own Ritual

The rituals suggested in this story could be used for a variety of purposes—to release fears or sadness dealing with other losses, such as in relationships or moving. Although these sound like very different reasons to use the balloons, there is loss in every transition, an ending in each new beginning.

One caution: Balloons are a health hazard for water fowl, fish, and other creatures who may ingest the popped rubber. Releasing them with a pin contains the balloon waste and also provides the main participant with the emotional release needed to heal.

17
Abortion

Sinking Stone

You slipped between my legs
like a blot of sun.
The thought of you
remains in me
like a sinking
stone,
You sink
beneath the waves
like a stone of sun.

Carla was staring out the window of her apartment. The curtain flapped
a little and a candle next to the bed flickered in the breeze. Her mind raced
through the options open to her as she studied the curtain's rhythm. Her
emotions were caught in her throat, her stomach tied in knots from her
phone call with Ray.

She had told him about their pregnancy. It was clear that he was
not happy about it. They were both in school. She had one more semester
before she got her bachelor's degree. Then she was planning on graduate
school, which was necessary in order to get a job in her field. They had
never talked of marriage. Ray was due to move away; he was beginning an
internship that would take him to another state at the end of January. It was
August; he wouldn't even be here when the baby was due.

This was clearly not the time for her to get pregnant. They had
used birth control, but something hadn't worked. With Ray's reaction and
her impending graduation, she knew what she had to do. She was also
worried about the implications for their relationship.

Her mind raced from Ray to the fetus. She had been to several parties recently and had had her share of wine and beer. Carla worried about
whether the baby was healthy or not. At that thought, her tears flowed
heavily.

The phone rang and she let the answering machine pick it up. Her
friend Jeanie was on the line.

"Carla, I wanted to know how you were doing. Have you talked to Ray yet? Are you all right?"

Carla picked up the phone. "Jeanie?" Then she broke into sobs.

"I'll be right over," Jeanie said.

When she arrived, Carla told her the whole story. "Do you think I'm crazy? I feel so confused."

"Not at all," Jeanie replied. "When I had an abortion I wish I had done it all differently. If I had to go through that again, I'd have a ceremony to help us work out all the feelings that came up, I'd have some way of completing with the spirit of the child, and I'd include the man as much as I could. This isn't just your problem, Carla. You and Ray could do something together that would help both of you let go and move on."

Just then the doorbell rang. Ray's voice came across the intercom: "Carla, I'm sorry. I acted like a fool on the phone. Let me in—we need to talk."

As Carla and Jeanie waited for Ray to come upstairs, Carla asked Jeanie if she would stay and discuss her idea with Ray. Maybe he would be open to it.

Ray hugged Carla and apologized for abandoning her in the middle of a crisis. "I know this is our problem, and I want to be here in whatever way I can," he said.

Carla was glad to see him and hear his change of attitude. "Ray, Jeanie is here—I asked her to stay; she has helped a lot, and she has an idea that I think will help us both." Ray was surprised to see Jeanie, but she was a friend to both of them, and he welcomed her presence.

The three sat down together. Jeanie shared her experience of how she would have done things differently.

"I was about to tell Carla about a ritual I read about," she said. "It was a way to help this couple work through their pain after a miscarriage. First they shared their feelings and cried together. Then they talked to the spirit of the child." I think you two could do something similar, before or after the procedure. Whatever you decide to do."

"Ray, let's do it together," said Carla. "I need to do this together."

Ray looked at Carla for a long time. "Okay, I think it sounds like something that would help us both. Can we do it now?"

Carla looked at Jeanie in surprise at Ray's enthusiasm, and they agreed this was a good time. Carla got up and brought the candle from the bedside to the table. Then she got a scarf that had belonged to her grandmother. She also retrieved an egg-shaped stone that was lying on the dresser.

"My grandma was so wise; she would have helped me in the best way she could if she were still here. Maybe she could be here now in spirit."

Carla laid the scarf on the table, under the candle, and placed the stone there too.

"Jeanie, please lead us through this," Carla asked.

Jeanie took a deep breath and reached for their hands around the table. "I ask that the highest and wisest good be present for all of us. We ask to surround ourselves in light. May the kindest and wisest spirits be present, including Carla's grandmother, and the spirit of this little person who wants to come through." Jeanie picked up the stone egg. "Let's use this to help us take turns." She handed the egg to Carla.

Carla began to cry. "I feel so sad that this is happening now, just when I'm about to finish school. I'm not ready to be a mother."

Then she straightened herself and stared at the candle. "Little One, I hope you can hear me. I respect the fact that you want to come through us into this world. But this is not a good time for you to come. I want a family someday—but not now. If I don't finish school first, I won't be able to support myself, let alone you. I'd have to go on welfare, or have some job that I hate. That is not how I want to live my life, nor what I want for you or the rest of my family. Little One, I want the best for you and I can't give you anything unless I finish what I have started. I ask that you not come now, please; this is not the right time." She placed the egg in the center of the table.

Carla felt as though she were talking directly to the child who wanted to be born. Her tears streaked her face; her eyes were fixed on the candle.

Ray picked up the egg and said quietly, "I ask the spirit of this child to wait—wait until we can provide for you. I would like a family, too, but neither Carla nor I can be there for you now. Please, I ask that you find parents who can care for you."

Then Ray took Carla's hand. "I'm sorry you have to go through this. I'm sorry for the way I treated you on the phone. I want you to know that I'll be there through the abortion. I love you, Carla. Please forgive me."

Carla was still crying, and squeezed Ray's hand. He passed the egg to Jeanie.

"I'm so grateful for this time together. It helps me with the pain left from my abortion. It is a difficult choice that you two are faced with. I ask for the best possible outcome for each of you. I also want to say to the

100

child whom I had to let go of—please forgive me. I hope you find parents who want you and can care for you. I ask for help with forgiving myself." Jeanie placed the egg in the center of the table. "If anyone has anything else to say, just pick up the egg."

Carla slowly moved her hand across her grandmother's scarf and put her fingers around the egg. As she drew it closer she looked at Ray. "I'm glad you apologized. I hope we can keep talking together more honestly. I forgive you for abandoning me in all this. I still love you. I don't want this to break us up—maybe it will bring us closer together. I'm so glad you're here now; it makes a big difference."

Then she turned to Jeanie. "Thank you for helping us create this ritual together. I ask for the best possible outcome for all of us." As Carla put the egg back in the center of the table, Ray and Jeanie took her hands and the three of them sat silently for a moment.

The next day Carla felt cramping in her abdomen. By that evening she had started bleeding, and felt the fetus pass. She called her doctor to get further instructions. Then she called Ray and Jeanie.

That night she and Ray lit the candle by her bed. The two of them watched the flame as they held the cold stone egg in their interlocking fingers. "Thank you, Little One," Ray said quietly. "I hope you find a good home where you are loved and wanted."

"Yes, thank you, thank you," Carla echoed.

Creating Your Own Ritual

Perhaps your circumstances are not the same as Carla and Ray's. You may have had an abortion ten years ago and still have unresolved feelings. You may have had to go through the experience completely alone, without supportive people to stand by you.

Here are two suggestions that may help you after the fact, whether you had the procedure last week or five, ten, or twenty years ago.

Make a list of friends or family members whom you would like to join you in a rite of letting go. Select only those people who can be with you without judgment and without trying to fix you. Give yourself time to consider the list carefully. It need not be a long one—one or two friends may be enough. After selecting an appropriate time for the ritual, ask your friends to join you.

Gather in a circle, then pass burning sage or cedar around, so everyone gets the smoke flowing in and around them. You may want to burn sage in a bowl, called smudge, or smoke the whole room before you start.

Next, tell your story of what you experienced before, during, and after the procedure. Let the emotions out and say whatever you need to about the events surrounding the abortion. During the ceremony be sure to ask for what you need. If you wanted to have someone hold your hand during the abortion but no one did, be sure to have someone in the circle do it now. If you need to cleanse yourself of the memories, use some water in a bowl to wash you face or hands, or ask someone to do it for you.

Be sure to express whatever unexpressed feelings you have. When you feel complete, invite any of the participants to share their feelings. You may be surprised how many others have experienced similar losses. When you are finished sharing, complete the circle by thanking each of your supporters. You may want to give them each a gift for being there for you. Perhaps you can share a meal afterward.

Another suggestion is similar to the balloon release ritual (discussed in chapter 10). Buy some white balloons filled with helium and divide them in half. Pop half the balloons for regrets or sorrows, and half for blessings for the spirit of the unborn child. You may want to pop most of them and then let one go, perhaps at night during a full moon.

18
Purification

Phoenix Blue

Oh! You match the sky!
I see through your eyes
to the clouds
drifting with ease.
The sun catches each random form.

You know every cloud holds rain.
One circles like a hawk,
reminding you of another storm

which destroyed your house
and made the phoenix rise.

Now you let the clouds
pass by and nothing is held
in the sky too long.

Transparent blue,
clouds floating,
In your eyes
they pass
right through you.

Phoenix Lake is like a small jewel in the middle of Marin County. My friend Julie and I were hiking around it, talking about the next steps for both of us. Her life was as full as mine was solitary. She had a love affair, and a job that involved working with many people. She scarcely had enough time to eat and sleep regularly. I was beginning to think about being in a relationship again after having cloistered myself for several years in an attempt to know myself better and to help give birth to my writing. Our walk gave her some quiet time, and me companionship.

A few weeks before our walk, Julie and I had been discussing some of the rituals I had created. She had asked to participate in one when the time came. I told her I wasn't sure when I would need one again, but I would let her know. Her request gave me time to step back from my life and consider the next steps.

My solitude was getting lonely. I knew there were many things that I couldn't learn unless I was in a relationship. I also felt drawn to cleanse myself from past relationships in order to mark a new beginning. It was as though I needed a bath.

On the walk around Phoenix Lake, Julie and I talked about relationships, the need for purification, and about what it means to start over. I had told her the ritual was to help me create a new beginning.

"Where do you want to do the ritual?" she asked as we started on the path.

"I don't know, somewhere around this lake; the name seems so appropriate. I think I'll know the place when we get there," I replied.

Halfway around the lake the trail took a turn and dipped over a rise. It moved down the hill and over a creek by way of a bridge to a place surrounded by redwoods. The water was clear at the bottom of the stream and fairly shallow. I was delighted.

"This is the place!" I said, smiling. Julie looked as surprised as I was sure, and followed me down to the stream bed.

An old tree stump lay just under the water's surface. There were pebbles and stones around it. The water was cool. "I need you to be a witness for me, Julie," I said quite seriously.

"Okay, anything you say, Rob," she responded. I stood on the log and found that my heals fit right into two depressions. My feet were about a foot apart. I squatted down close to the water, looking at the stones. Just as I leaned over, a man came bounding down the trail. I was startled, and smiled at him, feeling that his appearance was somehow very symbolic. He disappeared around the bend as fast as he had arrived. "It seems everything is part of this rite," Julie said with a smile.

I reached across to a spoon-shaped stone that seemed to be laid there just for me, and picked it up and giggled. Julie said softly, "Oh, I see you use what's at your fingertips." I just nodded and smiled in acknowledgment. The water gurgled around my ankles. I felt like a playful five-year-old, fascinated with what lay around my feet. I closed my eyes for a moment to listen for what needed to happen next.

A prayer rose from deep inside me. "Great Spirit, I am your daughter. I ask that this water cleanse me, I ask for healing and purification, and I honor my friend Julie who is a witness to my request." At that I took the spoon and splashed water between my legs four times. One for each of the directions. I had a skirt on, so the water hit my underwear with a cool splash. I enjoyed the feeling of the breeze and the water on my skin.

My legs felt as though they were two thin trees coming right out of the old log. I looked at Julie and closed my eyes. "Thank you, Great Spirit." I splashed the cool water over my face and head. "It is done." It was all I needed to do.

As I stood up, a group of women walked out of the woods and a man ran past us. They were unaware of what we were doing in the creek; perhaps they thought we were looking for frogs. I smiled at the thought.

Julie and I hopped back on the trail. The sky seemed more blue to me, with only a few clouds reflected in the lake. Everything around us looked vibrant. We walked in silence, experiencing our new feelings.

After a while Julie said, "That was so simple, and yet quite profound. I feel a shift inside me."

"We'll talk later," I said. "I just want to enjoy this new space I'm in." She smiled in acknowledgment, and we walked back to the car in silence. As we drove home I wondered who this new man was whom I was about to meet.

Reflecting on Purification

With the exception of baptism, to my knowledge there are no rituals in our culture that address purification. As a form of renewal it can mark beginnings in relationships and within our own being.

In many tribal traditions, purification for both men and women is part of annual cycles. In the Native American tradition sweat lodges, like a sauna, are a common method of purifying the body. The sweat lodge is a ceremony, however, and takes place once a month, or during the spring and fall equinoxes or summer and winter solstices. Smoke from burning small sage or cedar boughs is used before many Native American ceremonies. The sage cleanses the air whereas the cedar is thought to affirm positive energy. The process is called smudging.

In India incense has been used to purify the air. It also sets the mood for meditation and deeper communion with spirit.

For me purification has become a necessary part of my spiritual practice. Whether I partake of monthly sweat lodges or annual spring retreats, bathe in streams, or smudge from time to time, I always feel renewed and ready to start again.

As women we have the advantage of nature helping us remember to rest and cleanse through our menstrual cycle. Several ways that friends and I take the opportunity to slow down and realign ourselves with nature during menses are explored in chapter 6, "Menses and Sexuality."

19
Menopause

Moon Circle

In honoring one,
We regard all
Maiden, Mother, Crone,
each one unique
all from one
never
ending
river
of
moonlight.

Marlene was standing in a circle of women she had invited. The air was warm and the day sunny. The gathering was a large one, and she welcomed the support, honoring her waning moontime, her entry into what she named her crone years.

"I'm glad to see all of you here. As you know, this is a ritual honoring my crone initiation. Originally the wise woman, the crone was considered very powerful, the highest council. We are honoring the original interpretation of crone with this rite. I want this to be a celebration not only for me today, but for all of us as wise council for each other.

"We are going to be mixing traditions today. Since I have lived in Africa, South America, and the United States, I felt the need for all these traditions to be represented. I've given each of you a sheet listing the day's events; just follow along, and enjoy yourselves!"

Marlene left the circle and walked to the alter behind her and lit a candle with three flames. The number three had been in her dreams. Three—the triangle; the sacred "delta of Venus"; ancient sign of feminine power; maiden, mother, and crone, the three stages of a woman's life— these images appeared over and over in her dreams. She had fasted for three days before the rite, and now this number would be used symbolically throughout the day. She began by lighting the candle with three flames.

She brought the candle into the center of the circle. Her friend

Adriana went to the alter, picked up a shell with sage in it, lit it, and smudged each woman in the circle. Then two other women took a bowl of rose petals and some flowers from a vase. Each woman was sprinkled with rose petals and given a flower as others played drums, rattles, and other musical instruments. As her friends rejoined the circle, Marlene started a Seneca Indian chant to the moon, called "Nissa," from a tape by Rashini called Keeper of the Mysteries. Next a song called "Oh, Great Spirit" was sung, Then one of Marlene's friends sang a Tewa Indian prayer called "Song of the Sky Loom."

After the songs, four women did an invocation of the four directions. As each direction was invoked, chimes were sounded.

Marlene stepped forward and announced that she had been given an African name on her last visit to Nigeria. "My new name in Nigerian is "Ugonna—the Good One." To me it is my spirit name. As I say it again I'll ask you to repeat it back to me. "Ugonna!" Marlene said in a clear voice.

"Now, I invite each of you to state your name and, if you have one, your spirit name. The rest of us will sing your name back to you."

As each woman spoke, the others echoed her name back. Several more songs were sung, honoring the grandmothers, and great women and goddesses from every tradition, including Mary, Diana, Isis, Ashtar, Hecate, Demeter, Kali, and Innana. An African greeting song was sung next, as the women greeted each other. When they were
 through, Marlene held a giveaway, where she gave gifts to those who came, in the Native American Northwest Coast tradition.

In the garden adjacent to the friend's house where the ceremony took place were several large sculptures of major goddesses. The women were invited to move from station to station and meditate on each one. Several women who had done research on the goddesses gave information at each sculpture as they went.

The women entered the house for the second part of the rite. Marlene invited everyone to share a story from their life experience as a maiden, mother, or crone. She had a hoop set up as a loom, and a basket of yarn and cloth. Everyone was invited to weave their favorite colors into the loom as they spoke.

For the third part of the rite, Marlene was taken to an upstairs room by three women whom she had chosen to be her elders. They asked her two questions: "What are you letting go of today?" and "What are you invoking for yourself?" Then they spoke her new name. They bathed her in rose-scented water and dressed her in new white robes. They gave her bits of wisdom from three ancient traditions—African, Native American, and earth-based traditions in Europe. They told her secrets that remain so even now. When they were done with her initiation, they presented her to the women waiting downstairs, stating her name, Ugonna, as her friends formed a long tunnel through which she passed. Then they sang together in Spanish "Yo Soy Mujer" (I Am a Woman), a song written by Maria Del Valle and Mildred Bonilla.

To conclude the day, the women shared a pot luck feast; everything tasted especially good. Marlene broke her three-day fast. Many of the women gave her gifts to commemorate her rite of passage.

Through the next several months Marlene felt the shift in consciousness as she moved through her life. She felt that the rite was a gateway through which she had stepped into more wholeness, into more of herself as a woman.

Creating Your Rite of Menopause

The ritual Marlene created was purposely elaborate to celebrate womanhood with a large group of friends. Yours need not be so involved. If only a few friends or family members attend, it can be just as powerful as a daylong event.

The more thought and feeling you put into your rite, the more you will get out of it. This doesn't mean it has to be complex; on the contrary—it can be simple, spontaneous, and still very powerful. You can choose to prepare in days, weeks, or months. The choice is yours.

The following are some basic suggestions for a crone ritual.

Review old family pictures or other records you may have that remind you of the past. Give yourself some time to do this. You may want to take each decade in a month. If you are doing your rite at fifty, sixty, or seventy, you could use five, six, or seven months for this review. Perhaps you could make an album or scrapbook of the highlights.

Cleaning out rooms of your house, as a metaphor for cleaning out your life, can be a way to 'take inventory' and release what is no longer needed. It clears the way for embracing the future.

Consider friends and family whom you would like to attend. Perhaps there are those whom you consider to be elders. See if they would be open to creating a rite with you or if they would attend one that you created. If your elder(s) or grandparent(s) have passed away, you can incorporate memories and stories about their lives that exemplify their gifts to you. Reminiscing happens naturally at family gatherings—why not create an event so more people can participate?

Fasting is an ancient way of preparing yourself for a transition. It can be done for a day or so before the rite to prepare yourself. Unless you have specific health problems for which fasting is not advised, such as diabetes, there are no ill effects. In fact, informed fasting can be very beneficial to your health; there are many good books on the subject.

Spend some time contemplating what it means to enter your wisdom time. You may have plans for retirement, or there may be new adventures on the horizon.

Listen within for guidance on what you need to do in this ritual. Do not discount ideas that seem out of the ordinary. Share them with a friend you trust to see how they sound.

You may want to incorporate your photo album or other mementos as the first part of the ritual, your plans and dreams as part of the second phase, and, as the third part, a ritual bath or fresh clothes, as in Marlene's rite. These simple acts can be a powerful metaphor for transition. If you are not comfortable with the ritual bath, leave it out or take it privately while your friends sing or chant for you. Special foods can be prepared for your feast, which you can do alone or with friends and family. Stories from your elders can be incorporated in last portion of the rite. Maybe they have blessings for you or gifts to share that symbolize the strength, love, and wisdom they have gained along the way.

You will know what you need to do. Just listen to your intuition and let your imagination guide you.

SECTION THREE

HONORING PERSONAL TRANSITIONS

20
Starting Over

A Birthday Celebration

Burning Field

We set the field afire
and watched the burning
you at one end,
I at the other.
We called to each other
and watched a deer take flight,
but never met in the cool river
where fire could not burn us.

Instead, our passion singed the air
with blackness
and we destroyed the homes
of countless tiny creatures.

At dusk, we met
in the center of the field
and found ourselves standing
on the crisp bones of a fawn.

Sometimes it is necessary to be leveled, like taking a field down to the soil to replant. No one could say that it happens at the same age for everyone. Growth happens at any time. I experienced the beginning of such a leveling in my early thirties. Because the changes seemed inevitable, I decided to honor this time by surrendering to it instead of fighting what I could not control.

The age of thirty-three was very special for me because I was born on the third of January. Some people call the birthday that is the same as the date of birth your golden birthday. Thirty-three was my double golden birthday! Through some interest in numerology I had learned about numbers that were significant for me. Three was my number of lessons, where-as four was a number of completion. I could sense, with the way events were unfolding for me, that there were difficult times ahead. It seemed as good a time as any to honor this impending year of lessons with some sort of special ritual.

I was living on a farm in Michigan, which is almost always very cold and snowy in January. This particular year was no different. Regard-less of the weather, I had decided that on my birthday I would hike to the sauna in the woods and spend my birth time in the middle of a pine forest where I could pray and meditate.

I was born in the middle of the night, so I got up at around two in the morning to begin my hike. The snow was not too deep, as we were in the middle of a thaw, so the temperature hovered around twenty degrees. Upon my arrival at the site, I split the wood and lit the fire for my ritual cleansing.

The sauna sat at the edge of a cornfield next to a winding creek. The structure looked like an old log cabin with two rooms inside and a front porch. The first room had benches and hooks on the wall for chang-ing clothes. The second room had a woodstove and two levels of benches along the walls like built-in bunk beds. There was enough room inside for four adults to lie on each bench. The room was highly insulated on all four sides, so it got very hot, even in the coldest weather.

When I arrived that night, the sauna was damp inside and the fire was not easy to light. I dropped into a deep awareness that lighting the fire was the beginning of the ritual. I was relearning the value of tenacity and perseverance while I coaxed the fire along. A sacred feeling enveloped me. I realized there were lessons for me with every step if I could only slow down and listen.

Once the fire was lit I walked to the nearby river and dipped a bucket between plates of ice where the water still flowed freely. While waiting for the sauna to heat up, I sat in the outer cabin and hummed songs that came to me. I felt very old and very childlike at the same time, rock-ing back and forth to various tunes.

Something in my Scandinavian ancestry seemed to come alive in the sauna. I felt so connected with the earth and all of life. This was the first time I was taking a sauna alone, and it felt very important to be mark-ing my birth in this way. When the room was hot enough, I stripped down and jumped inside. I sweated until I couldn't tolerate it anymore, then ran outside in the snow where the icy bucket of river water waited. After dowsing myself with cold water, I jumped back into the sauna, repeating the process three times, one for each decade of my life. At the end of the last round, I put my clothes back on and, without dousing myself again, walked toward the deepest part of the woods.

It was very dark at three-thirty in the morning, even with the moon. Only the owls were awake. The woods were especially scary. However, I loved these woods and knew the trails well. I also knew that if I gave into my fear, it would be horrifying. If I prayed and stayed in a positive frame of mind, it would be an enriching experience.

Soon I reached the spot where I had spent many hours listening to the birds and praying during walks in the woods. Tall pine trees towered above me. Moss lay under the snowy patches. I spread out a blanket that my grandmother had made for me, and took my clothes off again. I was still steaming from the sauna. The cool night air felt good on my skin. I was not cold at all. I looked all around me, straining to see any sleeping deer. It seemed as though I was alone.

That night I prayed that the coming year would teach me the lessons that I needed to learn. A shiver raced up my spine; I knew these lessons would not be easy. I prayed for the faltering relationship that was ending in my life. It was important to me that both of us grow toward our highest good, even though I was very sad that what we shared together was dying. I prayed for my relatives and close friends who were also going through rough times. I stayed until the night air began to feel cold on my skin and I could see a hint of light through the tree branches.

To my surprise several deer began to stir not far from where I was sitting. They were so close I could hear their morning groans as they stretched and sleepily walked out of the woods toward the field. Knowing they were that close throughout my vigil seemed very comforting to me. It was a graceful feeling I remembered throughout the rest of the year. When I felt complete with my prayers, I got dressed again, wrapped myself in my blanket, and headed for the house. It was an amazing mystical night in the woods.

The following year was indeed filled with difficult experiences. It was a time when my life was completely changed. The relationship I was in ended, as I feared it would, signifying the end of home, family, and security to me. I had tried to make my living as an artist, which proved impossible. I was discovering that visual art was not solely my life direction. Money was scarce. I had lived out all my dreams and found none of them fulfilling or sustaining. I felt deep despair and emptiness, and had no idea what to do next.

Slowly by the end of the year, after therapy, several support groups, and help from friends and family, I was beginning to feel my feet under me again. By the following year the personal work I had done paid off, and I made a significant recovery. It was the most difficult year of my life and I survived. I may have survived without my deep woods experience, but the ritual helped me regain balance in the midst of chaos. Most of all, it helped me bow to the coming changes instead of resist them.

My woods experience was the calm place for me in the eye of the hurricane. Throughout that year, I remembered the peace alone in the sauna and the prayers I had made in the woods. I remembered the deer and the gift of their presence that cold morning.

Between those towering pine trees where I had prayed, I had affirmed my trust in the cosmos or God or whatever you choose to call it. Just as there was a reason to walk into the dark woods alone, I had a reason for being alive, even though I wasn't sure what it was yet. That night I had taken the first handful of seeds and scattered them over the scorched field.

Creating Your Own Ritual for Beginning Again

It may not appeal to you to venture out into the woods naked and alone in the middle of winter, and I am not suggesting you try it. However, this section is designed to support your inward journey. Acknowledging pain is the first step toward healing, and birthdays can be, at times, very difficult transitions. They can also be a good opportunity to release the past and start again. In painful times a retreat can be more beneficial than a party.

The second step is to find others to help you. If your birthday feels like the end of chapter in your life, look into support groups and twelve-step programs, or find a counselor who can help affirm your positive qualities and look at what you need to change. Counselors can give the emotional support you need during difficult times.

Your birthday rite may look very different from mine. Perhaps you prefer to have a group of friends over and create a transition that is more celebratory. (See chapter 8 for some inspiration for that approach.)

Whether you decide to go off alone or create a birthday ritual with friends, you can use your birthday as a turning point for change and renewal. Begin with a few guidelines that may clarify your needs and help you form your birthday rite:

1. Make a gratitude list. Take as much paper as you need. Your rite can begin here, acknowledging those you invite as friends who have supported you, if you choose others to be present.

2. Next reflect on your life story, citing the events and circumstances that have brought you thus far. You may want to highlight them for the beginning of your rite.

3. Make a second list releasing the past. These may be people you need to forgive, ways of being that don't work anymore, or places in your past that need to be let go. During the ceremony read the list of what you want to release, then burn it.

4. Then ask yourself what qualities, such as patience, compassion, and forgiveness, you want to develop more fully within yourself. You can use water, perfume, or ash from the burned release list to adorn and bless yourself with each new quality during the ceremony.

5. You can always end your ritual with this prayer: "This or something better, whatever is for my highest good." This sets your intention for right action, surrender, and the best possible outcome.

6. Ask for help if you need it. Knowing you are not alone can be such a relief. Others will be happy to help if you simply ask.

21
Career Changes

Becoming

I want to rise like a spark
from a fire straight to the stars.
I want to become a poem, a star,
shining like a firefly.

I want to become a word
spoken softly with power,
a word like "open" but with more blazing,
a word like "only" with less longing,
one word where all other words pause.

And when I know the word,
I will speak it once
and write it down with black ink,

only one word.

There are some things no one can prepare you for, like the impact of changing careers. I had no idea the transition would take several years, along with every bit of strength and focus I could muster. The problem was that I didn't just want a job—I wanted to live out my purpose for being alive. I knew that writing and practicing massage were aspects of that future, but I had no way of knowing how to make them work financially. I wanted to help myself through the next phase of my life with as little difficulty as possible.

After graduate school I took a job doing administrative work in San Francisco. I had no intention of staying in the position permanently. In fact, after eight months I was getting strong messages from my intuition that I should quit, yet I had no idea how I would support myself. I felt very apprehensive about the future.

My life for the past four or five years had already been filled with nonstop change. I had left a career in the museum field, divorced, relocated cross-country, completed graduate school, and moved my belongings and studio several times in the process. I was not enthusiastic about more change. Just as I was mulling over how to go about it all, a friend called, inviting me to a small gathering of friends from graduate school. We were each to bring something to share about what we had been doing since we left school and tell our dreams for the future. It seemed like a perfect opportunity for me to receive some support.

When I feel stuck I resort to one of my mottoes: When all else fails, clean out your files. Basic organizing seems to help me lay the groundwork for inflow and output of information. This time I concentrated on the files labeled résumés, art exhibits, and catalogs—the ones from my days as a curator and artist. I took the exhibit catalogs that I had created for the museum, flyers of exhibits I had participated in, news clippings of shows, résumés, and whatever else I could find that represented my previous life, and stuffed it all in a paper sack. I was attempting to let go of everything that had to do with past career directions.

For several months before my friend's timely call, I had been working on a large painting of the goddess Kwan Yin, goddess of love and compassion. Kwan Yin is a female deity in Japanese and Chinese Buddhism who really drew my attention. By making a painting of her depicting my face and hands, I intended to develop a more compassionate attitude toward myself. Although I did not follow the Buddhist tradition, I found myself collecting photos and sculptures of her.

Kwan Yin became the antidote to my raging inner critical choir which I could not seem to quell. My painting of her helped me become more aware of a supportive internal voice. By shifting from positive to negative thoughts, I could be more objective about the negative ones. Then I personified the voices by drawing pictures of the characters as a way of understanding myself better. Psychologists call these various aspects of the self "subpersonalities."

It became a serious game of hide-and-seek. One after another in meditation, I could hear distinct characters. Then I tried to draw them. The characterizations helped me to isolate and clarify these parts of myself, thus reducing their impact on me. It became an ongoing ritual to understand myself.

One I named Lizzy Borden. She was the silent, deadly woman who, out of the blue with a slip of her knife, said hurtful things to people. As I listened to her I realized that she was actually trying to protect my creativity by alienating others. The underlying belief I held at the time was that I couldn't be in relationship and be creative. I also had a desire not to hurt those I love. Through Lizzy I became aware of a serious internal conflict.

To resolve this conflict the wiser Kwan Yin showed Lizzy what she was doing. Lizzy was transformed into a protector of my creative boundaries by letting me know first when it was time to withdraw from others so that I could write, draw, or paint before I felt overrun. Kwan Yin also helped voice my needs with love and understanding, so I could draw boundaries without hurting others.

Then there was Mac, the truck driver, who was extremely bull-headed. He disregarded the gentler characters that were getting run over by him. Externally it showed up as willfulness. By listening to Mac I realized he was afraid of getting bulldozed himself. I also discovered much gentler parts of myself that were getting squashed by him. So I gave the road kill a voice, and Mac learned what damage he was doing. Because he was really a big guy with a soft heart, I made him the protector of the endangered species. This transformed him from murderer to protector of my internal environment. Externally in relationships with others, I began to listen better and express my viewpoint without so much will and with more compassion.

There were many other characters. Some were members of my own family who had been critical of me at vulnerable times in my development as a child. Sometimes I needed sessions with professionals, who guided me with hypnotherapy or other techniques. Through a variety of processes, internal conflicts transformed into resolution. Kwan Yin was the overseer. The journey was simultaneously difficult, humorous, and healing.

As Kwan Yin loved each and heard his or her story, I realized that all the characters were actually trying teach me something in their own way. Once I heard their messages, and identified the beliefs that supported their behavior, I could change that belief through positive affirmations. The characters then changed and became integrated into the folds of Kwan Yin's robes, joining a single positive voice that was more supportive. As each became part of the whole, I burned the drawings one by one when I was ready to release them. I felt very grateful for the creative process.

Kwan Yin was hanging on my wall, but I couldn't seem to finish her. One friend commented that I hadn't stepped into the robes yet. In the two weeks before the party, I was determined to finish the painting. She became the centerpiece of the ritual I was about to devise.

The party was at Ann and George's house. It was a beautiful place—just what I needed to help me feel more grounded and at home.

George and Ann and my other friends from school were warm and loving; it was wonderful to see them again.

The school we attended was used by many of us as a launchpad for creative projects. This gathering was a 'show and tell' night for us. After we shared a potluck dinner, each of us talked about our life and what we were doing. Some brought paintings and others showed pictures or read stories they had been writing. I chose to be last. I wasn't sure how long the ritual would take, and I didn't want to monopolize the time we had together. I also felt as vulnerable as I had with "Feather and Claw." This time I had a different community of friends and a focus for my future.

The group took a little break while I got set up. George and I hung Kwan Yin on one wall while we cleared another wall to show slides of a selection of my paintings from my past. Then I emptied the paper sack and laid out all the flyers, catalogs, and résumés on the floor in a semicircle, placing two candles in the center at the feet of Kwan Yin. I wore a kimono which seemed perfect for the occasion.

When I was ready and the group was ending the break, I said a few words about what I was going through and explained that I wanted them to witness my surrender to my future. Before I could go on I had to let go of the past, which included my former careers as an artist and curator. I told them they would be seeing slides of my work on the screen. The rest of the ritual they would understand.

As the slides began to click one at a time, I knelt down on the floor, lit the candles, and sorted through the flyers and catalogs, making two piles—one of mementos and one to throw away. I took time to consider each one. As I finished sorting, the slides were still going. I sat and watched them flash by one by one. Each slide brought memories with it, some happy, some sad. All in all, the process helped me let go of the past, and embrace my new self.

When the slides were over, I asked if there were any questions or comments. Some people, having known me less than two years, said they had no idea what I did before I came to California. They were delighted to see my work and hoped I would continue painting as well as writing. I said I felt that writing and massage were the two things I wanted to do more than paint, but that I would continue to paint if the mood struck me. I was giving up the professional aspects of art. Others commented on the "feeling tone" during the ritual. (By feeling tone I mean the sense of awareness or shift in your inner knowing—a realization or "Aha" that comes across.) They could sense something shift in the room as I completed sorting everything. Needless to say, so did I.

120

I thanked them for being such loving friends, witnessing a time of uncertainty. Once again I was grateful to have taken the time to create what I needed for an important transition.

A few weeks after Ann and George's party, I got a job doing massage at the Claremont Hotel and Spa, which had just opened six months prior. In the months that followed, I also began to work at the Nob Hill Club in San Francisco, and started a private practice as well. In my time between jobs and appointments, I wrote poetry and continued with this book. The ritual I did with my friends was the turning point.

Reflecting on Your Career Changes

Over the past twenty years recent studies show that Americans change careers an average of three times during their life. This makes it likely that most people will experience a career change at some time during their life. There are many ways to help yourself make the transition more smoothly. A ritual can help.

Your career or occupation will largely determine the components of the ritual as well as the appropriate symbols. The objects you choose can represent your career and also the inner qualities you want to emphasize as you go through this time of change. A candle, for examples, represents inner knowledge and awareness; water symbolizes cleansing and flow. There are some important questions to consider:

* What are you letting go of?

* What do you want to do next? If you don't know the next steps, ask y   ourself what you love to do most. Could you make a living at it? Do you want to make a living at it? Talk to people who are doing what you want to do to see if the direction you are contemplating really suits you.

* Are there aspects of yourself that need to be listened to, let go of, or transformed before you make this transition? Perhaps there are fears that need to be addressed, or parts of yourself that need reassuring. As you work toward the goal of loving yourself into your new career, the ritual will, in part, create itself.

When you have listened to your needs and begun to act on them, you can address other questions, such as:

* How much money do you want to make?

* What kind of day do you want to have?

* How will this new direction contribute to others, the earth, yourself, and your family?

Once you've addressed these issues, gather the symbols of the past and the ones for the future. Then invite the guests.

22

A Dream Ceremony

The Noe Mask

A black and white mask
Over Dom's face
Restores balance.

I woke with my face covered in sweat. The image of Dominic's body and the Noe mask was as vivid as though I had just witnessed a murder. His body and the events of the dream whirled around in my head. He was a familiar member of my inner family, a part of myself out of control. As I felt the dream begin to fade, I grabbed a pen and wrote down the dream as if my life depended on it.

Dominic lay on his side with one black and one white gun next to his stomach and a Japanese black-and-white "Noe" theater mask over his face. The black and white and red blood flowed together. Under the mask an adolescent boy, thirteen—his life ending in violence. His mother came, mourning and wailing, his father with a young son, his younger sister—all came to view the body. The guns fit butt to nozzle, making a yin and yang symbol on the floor, resting in a pool of blood. They swirled like patterns of oil on water.

His name, Dominic, fit, for he dominated everyone in the family. Relief was mixed with sadness amongst his family. An adolescent—gone wild. He didn't care about anyone else, violent, deceptive, and willful. To his family, wild and creative; to the gang member who shot him, he had gone too far—stepped onto the turf of a rival gang, stealing their thunder, taking what did not belong to him. His death—the end of his games, deception, pranks, turmoil for the family.

In the living room—the family begins new life, new rules: tell the truth, care for one another. The younger children would be taught respect—care for themselves and other people.

This was no ordinary nightmare. A part of me had just died with Dominic. I had been initiated but I wasn't sure how or why. As I thought about the dream and what this represented, I realized that Dominic was a member of my inner family, one of many aspects of my self. He was a wild adolescent that did what he pleased. Although his actions were greatly exaggerated, there was the part of me that disregarded a healthy balance for creative explorations. I realized through the dream that under the mask was a lot of adolescent willfulness.

Although it was good to be creative, it was not good to throw the rest of my life out of balance in the process. I was in the midst of a powerful self-evaluation of the way I had operated in life up to that point. Before this dream my attitude had been "anything for art." In realizing the danger I put myself in over and over, I understood how my behavior caused me to suffer unnecessarily. The dream was a confirmation of the decision I had made a few days before.

In my waking life, I had worked hard for the summer on a project with a friend, working occasionally for money but barely making enough to survive. When the project was over, I needed to take time off to restore my energy—I was exhausted. I came back rested from time away, but with very little money and no savings. Just days before the dream, I had vowed never to stretch myself this thin again. It was too much. I would structure my time to provide for my needs before I went off on another wild-goose chase.

After writing down the dream, my first thought was to cement this death into my consciousness. I wanted to unveil the adolescent, shift my outer life to meet this initiation, and end these adolescent ways once and for all. The creativity was welcome but the disregard for the welfare of my health, financial stability, or my internal family was not.

When it was late enough in the morning, I called three friends and asked them to join me the next night in a ritual. Each agreed to participate, not knowing how or why they were involved. I really appreciated their curiosity and trust in me. I knew if I didn't "strike while the iron was hot," I would never do the rite.

Over the next forty-eight hours, I did some research on Japanese Noe theater masks and made a facsimile of one for the rite. I used what materials I had available. I glued tissue paper over a plastic milk bottle and formed eyebrows, a mouth, and a nose. I painted my mask white and black, resembling the one in the dream as closely as I could. Then I gathered the tools I needed to complete the ritual enactment of Dominic's death. The guns were made of cardboard and, as in the dream, resembled the yin and yang—the ancient Chinese symbol for the balance of masculine and feminine, black and white, earth and sky, the intuitive and the material, the known and the unknown. I cut tiny bits of red cloth to symbolize blood. I then gathered candles, a sheet to sit on, the story I had written from my dream, the mask, a cardboard yin and yang symbol that had the rough shapes of pistols, and two kimonos that I had in my closet, one for the father in the story, and one for the mother.

I thought about my research as I worked. Noe theater productions were originally tragedies performed by men. In the plays women who lost sons were depicted by men wearing long-sleeved kimonos, so they could wipe their tears. I was creating, in essence, a funeral–theater–performance piece ritual. I remembered from graduate school, when I traced theater to its roots, that the plays were originally ritual enactments of the human psyche and were a part of sacred festivals. I was returning to the roots of theater, art, music, and dance — all ancient ways to celebrate and compre-hend the divine in each of us.

When my friends, Lawrence, Lisa, and Clara, arrived we sat to-gether as I explained what we were going to do. I told them as little as pos-sible, but enough to make them comfortable with the transpiring events. I wanted to be sure that everyone knew I was not interested in reenacting Dominic's actual death, yet I wanted to preserve the element of surprise, allowing the ritual to unfold for them as a dream. I explained to them that they were here to help me shift my inner consciousness, making the dream more real in my waking life. The "death" had actually already happened within me. After everyone felt comfortable enough with the proceedings, and each person agreed to support me in reenacting my dream, we gath-ered the objects I had made and headed toward the basement door.

"Where are we going?" Lisa asked nervously.

"Shhh," I said, "just hold on to the person in front of you and fol-low me," We moved in silence through the dark basement of my house like an odd caterpillar. It seemed as though we were passing into the underworld. Outside in the yard the air was still. A waning moon gave us some light. I spread a sheet over the grass and we sat down in a circle. I put the tray of items in the middle. I gave them each a copy of the story of my dream with flashlights so they could see.

Each of them had a role or two in the dream. Lawrence represented the male aspect coming into balance; he was the father and the gang mem-ber who shot Dominic. Clara was the sister, and Lisa was Dominic. I was the mother who had to loose a son to gain balance within the family.

As I read the story, each person in the dream picked up their cues from the script I had written. The gang member (Lawrence) shoots Domi-nic (Lisa), places the Noe mask over his face, and sprinkles the red cloth bits over the mask. Each family member witnesses the body. Clara, Dominic's sister, took the guns and placed them on the tray handle to nozzle, forming a yin and yang symbol. The balance had been restored.

The four of us sat in silence for a moment. It had worked. I felt the shift inside my body. I could feel the dream-made-real settle into my cells. A slight breeze kicked up, and tiny red squares of cloth lifted off Lisa and blew onto the tray near the candles. She removed the mask from her head, and the ritual was over. I knew I would not throw myself out of balance to the point of exhaustion again. I felt this promise to myself becoming an unwavering part of my consciousness. The silent support from my friends surrounded me like the cool night air.

Creating Your Own Ritual from a Dream

Perhaps you have a dream that feels like a message to your waking self. Recording your dreams is easy. One suggestion is to keep handy a dream notebook or journal with a pen that works. Another is that as you are waking up, title your dream. This will help you remember the major images without losing the essence.

If your dream strikes you as an initiation, the rite I described can help you create your own. Your ritual enactment of a dream will depend on the images that come to you and what parts of the dream feel important to recreate and share with others.

Here are some guidelines to help you create your own ritual from a dream:

1. First, ask yourself what are the most powerful images in the dream. They will be the key to unlocking the new feeling tone (the sense of awareness or shift in your inner knowing) you may have, to helping you create the actual ritual. Once you have the images (for example, the mask, the blood, and the guns forming the yin and yang), you can begin creating the ritual.

2. Think of the dream as a story you wish to write. Play with it and don't be concerned if you have never done this before. This is not a Broadway production; it is a private play for you and a few others you may wish to include.

Perhaps writing a play or a story is not your medium. Try a song, or dance the new you, or simply invite some friends over to hear a poem you have written about such a dream. Remember, this is your rite and you can create it any way you choose. So long as your intention is to heal your spirit, there should be nothing to stop you from going for it.

3. Set the date and time for the rite. This is very important. Committing to a day helps you commit to carrying out the plan.

4. Invite your guests. Having witnesses often makes the shift more concrete for you. It also helps those friends or family closest to you understand how you have changed. If they have questions about what you're doing, offer to let them read this section of this book. It may help them create a rite of their own.

23
Rape Recovery

Reclaiming

Once you took from me the power
to choose,
to refuse,
to turn away and run.

Now I take it back,
breathe deeply,
stab your memory fiercely,
and banish you forever
from my dreams.

Jennifer carefully tied a large, clear crystal to one end of a bamboo pole. She painted the other end with several small stripes. Around the shaft she tied feathers with a thin strip of leather. As she worked she thought about her conversation with her classmate Pam the week before.

"I want to take back my power," Pam had said vehemently. "I want to feel my rage. I need to chase him back where he came from."

Jennifer replied, "I need something to attack him with. I want to confront my rage and the desire I have to kill him. Maybe we need to make spears—something to symbolize our own masculine power.

"Pam, maybe we need to do a ritual as part of our class presentation. We can talk about rape until we are blue in the face, but it doesn't touch the need I have to reclaim what was lost as a result of my rape. I need to embody my power again. I've never done a ritual like this before, but I have a sense of what I need to do. Maybe that's all we really need, to follow our instincts and use our creativity."

As they spoke, Jennifer and Pam began to realize that they could actually heal the feeling of being powerless. Both women had carried this sense with them since their rapes. They had each gone through a long healing process before they met, and were now ready for the final stage of their recovery. All they needed now was the intention to create a healing rite for themselves and a little preparation.

During the week they checked with the instructor of their "theory of art therapy" class to see if they could do the ritual as part of their final presentation. Their instructor thought it was a great idea. Next they began planning the ritual to reclaim their power. They also continued their research on rape. Because they were nearing the end of the semester, their reports were nearly finished. All that was left was to make their spears and gather the objects for the rite.

Jennifer tested the spear, thrusting it in the air a few times to make sure the crystal was tied securely. She looked carefully at all the surfaces of the stone and pole. She recorded every nuance of her own power object. Then she lit some sage in a shell and slipped the spear through the rising smoke. Now she was ready.

Their presentation took place during the last class of the semester. Jennifer entered the classroom, juggling her spear with her books and papers. Pam was already there, moving the chairs along the walls with the other students. Jennifer set down her things at one end of the room. The two women had not seen each other's spears before this class. Pam had hers in hand as she walked over to greet Jennifer.

"Look at how different our spears are, Jen." Pam held hers out for Jennifer to inspect. It was fierce looking, painted red with spines coming out of one end. Jennifer presented hers to Pam with an equal sense of accomplishment.

"We better get started," Jen said.

Jennifer began by outlining their presentation to the class. She let the class know that she and Pam had planned a ritual for the end of the class. Other students had the option to participate or not.

"If you don't want to participate," Pam continued, "we invite you to stay and act as witnesses. But we ask that once we begin the ritual, no one leave the room until the ritual is over. Please be aware that the ritual may bring up uncomfortable feelings for you. We want your participation at whatever level feels safe and right for you."

The two women took turns presenting the information they had collected on rape. Pam began:

"Thirty-three percent of all women have been sexually assaulted. Fifty percent of all suicide attempts are women who have been raped within the past year. Sixty percent of all female psychiatric patients have been raped."*23

Jennifer then outlined the four stages a woman goes through after she has been raped: "(1) crisis/disorganization, (2) pseudoadjustment, (3) reliving/depression, and (4) resolution/integration. As a conceptual tool,"

128

she explained, "these stages are not necessarily the same in all women. Often survivors will cycle through a few stages repeatedly before moving to the next."24 After outlining the stages, Jennifer spoke about creative arts strategies that can take place at each stage of recovery. She spoke of the importance of a personally meaningful ritual or rite of passage as a means of helping women through the aftermath of a rape.

When they were done presenting their research findings, Pam announced, "The ritual we are going to do is to help both of us find resolution and integrate our experiences of being raped. Those who want to participate can do so by coming to this end of the room and cheering on Jennifer and me."

She then explained other parts of the ritual, where the other participants would be involved. She asked those who did not feel comfortable to leave the room now. Only one or two people left; ten or twelve students witnessed from their desks. A few were the drummers. The remaining ten or twelve students formed a group at one end of the room. They would help contain the energy in the room and also help maintain the focused support Jennifer and Pam needed from the class.

When Pam was finished speaking and the students had settled into their places, she and Jennifer walked to the far end of the room. They put a chair at the center of the wall, placed a candle on the seat, and lit it. Then they walked to back to their starting place, where their supporters were waiting. They were glad to see several of the men in the class standing behind them. They looked down the narrow length of the room toward the candle. Both of the women picked up their spears.

After taking a deep breath and centering themselves, they looked at the members of the class who had volunteered to drum and nodded for them to begin. As the drums began to sound a steady rhythm, the two women slowly moved toward the candle. They held on to their spears tightly while thrusting them in the air, yelling and shouting. As they moved down the length of the room with the intention of jabbing their attackers, their supporters walked behind them, encouraging them on their way. Behind them they could hear shouts of, "Get him Pam," and, "Go for it, Jennifer!"

As the two women crossed the room, they screamed, "Get away from me! Get out of here! Go back where you came from! Get out! . . ." The intensity had been building, until the women stood near the chair, thrusting their spears at the flame, their faces streaked with sweat and tears.

When they stopped at the chair, they turned toward the candle flame, drawing upon the power inside them. They could feel the support of the community behind them. When they were ready, they simultaneously bent over and blew out the flame.

Slowly they turned toward their supporters, and the group formed a tunnel for them to pass through. Pam followed Jennifer though the maze without a word. When they reached the end of the tunnel, they turned toward the group, which had expanded into a circle. The rest of the class joined them, all facing the center.

Silently, Pam lead them in some simple movements. She touched her heart, and the class did the same. Then she and Jennifer stretched their arms overhead, extending their fingers. Each touched their thumbs and index fingers together, forming a triangle. Pam explained that this was an ancient symbol of feminine power.

The group followed their movements. They drew their triangles down their bodies, over their faces, and to their hearts. When they reached the heart, they flipped the triangle over with their index fingers pointing down, and continued the slow movement over their bellies and hips and down their legs. When they reached the floor the group moved their hands together so their little fingers touched, forming a circle of extended fingers and triangle shapes. Then, slowly, they raised the circle of fingers off the floor about a foot. Following Pam and Jennifer's lead, everyone leaned toward their triangle and blew air through its center, to blow life into the symbol of feminine power. Then Pam and Jennifer clapped their hands loudly, the group followed, and the ritual was over.

As everyone rose to their feet, Jennifer and Pam looked around the circle. They stood in silence for a moment, taking in the faces of their supporters. Many were in tears; others stood with their eyes closed, feeling the impact of the ritual, sweat dripping down their faces. The group spontaneously extended their arms around each other and stood for a moment in silence. Then the bell rang and it was time for the students to move to their next class.

As they moved to gather their things, classmates said they had not experienced anything like it. They were honored to participate and glad that Jennifer and Pam brought the theory to real practice in the classroom. Their instructor congratulated the women on a very moving presentation. Jennifer and Pam smiled as they picked up their spears, wiped their eyes, and moved to their next class.

Creating Your Own Ritual

Pam and Jennifer had the advantage of a class to support them in their ceremony. If you need a rite of this kind, perhaps a support group could act as the community for such a rite. In any case please note that Jennifer and Pam had done a lot of inner work before they were able to create this ritual for themselves. They had already worked through their denial and the outrage that stemmed from their experiences. Consult a counselor or rape crisis center if you need counseling assistance. They can help you determine where you are in your recovery, and also aide you in your healing process.

You will know whether you are ready to create such a rite for yourself. Listen to your aversions as well as your attractions to such a ritual. Pay attention to your dreams. Give yourself time to heal and process the incident. Seeking help from those trained to deal with such a crisis will help you fully meet the challenges of recovering from rape.

When you are ready, and you have a supporting group or individual whom you trust, imagine confronting your attacker. What do you need to do to take back your power? Notice the movements your body needs to make. Pay attention to what you need to say or shout at him. Go ahead and let yourself say it. Draw, dance, sculpt, or assemble an object to represent your power.

As you focus on your need to heal the feeling of powerlessness, you will sort out the details of your ritual. Looking at the final stage of rape recovery—resolution and integration—will give you some ideas for creating the ritual you need.

24
Moving Out

Shooting Star

This constellation,
though forever the same,
has shifted this winter.
Orion has invited one of us
to greet the sun.

Inge, Annie, and I had shared a house for four years. During that time we had gone through a lot of changes. Now it was time for Annie to move on. She had finished graduate school and was going to take some time to travel before returning to California.

Four years is a long time. We had a way of life together that seemed to work for us. We enjoyed one another as friends and appreciated each other's company, when we weren't dashing off in our individual directions. It became clear to me that we needed to do some kind of ritual in order to make this transition.

Before the appointed day, Annie needed a ride to drop off her car, which she had sold to provide extra money for her travel. She needed a ride to the bus from the new owner's house.

I followed her to their driveway and watched as she shut her car door for the last time and dashed for mine through the rain. When she hopped in, she put her hands over her face and began to cry.

"I love that car—I've had it for so long."

I touched her shoulder and said, "This is a big one, Annie."

"I know," she squeaked through her hands.

I thought for a moment, staring at the dash. Then I pulled some feathers out of the air vent. "Here, these are from a pheasant near my hometown. I think of them as blessing and protection. Take them and bless your car, Annie; say good-bye one last time."

She looked at them for a second and then stuffed them into her jacket and ran back to her car. I watched her through the streaks of water running down my car windows. She sat for a moment in her car. I could see her wiping it with the feathers. In the time it took me to turn my car around, she was finished. This time when she hopped in she was smiling, holding the feathers in her hand like a bouquet.

"I feel much better; that was perfect—thanks, Rob." She stuck the feathers back into the air vent, and we were off to the bus stop.

After a moment she said, "I'm glad we're doing our house ritual. I think we are all going to need it." I nodded in agreement.

Later that week the three of us gathered around our dining room table. Prior to the ritual we had talked casually about what we wanted to do. Inge wanted to go from room to room and talk about experiences we shared. I needed to do some grieving. Annie wanted to say some things to the two of us and share memories.

We began by lighting three candles, symbolizing each one of us. I placed a bowl of water and a small dish of salt next to the candles in the center of the table. We sat for a moment in silence.

"Well, do you want me to officiate?" I said softly, looking at my two friends. They nodded. I lit the candles and picked up the salt and poured it into the water.

"This is a little release ritual I learned from Starhawk. We stir the water counterclockwise for releasing or undoing, and say what it is we are letting go of. Then, when we are ready, we bless the water and stir it clock-wise, telling one another what we are taking with us. I'll start, if that's okay with the two of you." They nodded in agreement.

I drew the bowl close to me and watched the light play on the cut-glass edges. "I'm letting go of Annie as a roommate. I'm letting go of her as a live-in friend. Also our late-night talks and typing fits at our comput-ers, writing our hearts out, I am letting go. I'll miss our shared creative ventures and her cooking and . . . her stereo." We giggled together even though my face was wet with tears.

When I felt finished I pushed the bowl toward Inge. She looked at the water for a long time and slowly began to stir it with her finger.

"I'm letting go of Annie as a roommate but not as a friend," she be-gan. "I will think of you as part of the workshops we have done together. I will miss your cooking and our time together in the garden." When she was done she passed the bowl to Annie.

Annie, too, looked at the water for a long time. "I'm letting go of my room and bequeathing it to Robin. I'm letting go of our cat Monkey and giving him to Inge, now his full-time mom. I'm letting go of his sister Minka, too, and know Robin will take good care of her. I'm letting go of our noisy neighbors next door, also Mark and Judith downstairs, and my studio space in the basement." She continued for a few more minutes,

133

pausing between thoughts. When she was finished, she pushed the bowl back to me. I offered it again, in case anyone had something to add. Then, when we were complete, I pushed the bowl into the center of the table.

"Let's bless this water now," I said. We put our hands around the bowl.

"As I stir this water, we transform that which we are letting go of into that which we are taking with us." I stirred the water in a clockwise direction. After a few moments I pulled the bowl toward me and said, "I take with me the memory of our late-night talks and Annie's outrageous sense of humor . . ." I continued for a while with other memories. When I was through I slid the bowl to Annie.

"I will take with me the memories of this house, the sanctuary of my room. I take with me the friendships with both of you and the memories of our kittens when they first arrived. The friends we have entertained and our birthday parties . . ." Annie said.

Inge took her turn, and we passed the bowl once more for all the good times we shared together and separately. When we were finished we took up the candles and walked arm in arm to the kitchen and living room, into Inge's room, and to the bathroom, sharing memories as we went.

When we arrived in my room, I took a blue heron mobile from my bulletin board and said that I'd like to take it into Annie's room.

"Let's put it on the doorknob, Rob; I'm not out until Saturday," Annie said.

"No problem, that feels better to me anyway," I said, carrying it to her bedroom across the hall and placing it on the outer doorknob. We blew out the candles and hugged each other, feeling complete with our ritual.

A few days later Annie had taken the last of her things out of her room. She had moved the blue heron from the doorknob outside to the light cord in the center of my new room.

Creating Your Own Ritual

Whether you are married or single, moving your home can be a life-altering experience. Even if you move within the same town, your patterns of driving, the stores where you shop, and the people you see regularly are all subject to change. The farther away you move, the more difficult the transition.

Saying good-bye through ritual can affirm relationships on a heart-felt level. You honor the people who have meant the most to you. The rite can help release the emotions that may be rising and cresting. You take

134

time to adjust, grieve, and let go. The rite helps to integrate changes with more ease. It gives you an opportunity to release and mitigate some of the stress, mourning the past and embracing the future.

Moving into a new place can be fun, challenging, and equally stressful. The following chapter shows rites for moving in that can also ease that transition.

25
Moving In

Begin

Though time makes no difference,
there is a time
when all things begin.

It's in the timing,
one breath then another
and our paths unfold before us,
unfurl like flags,
one step at a time.

Then we may rise to the sun
or float up to the moon,
whichever you prefer.

For myself,
I choose the moon.
She knows my path,
and lights my way
with silver.

Annie's room was sunnier than mine had been and almost twice the size. As I stood in the center of her room—my new room—I began to fully appreciate the fact that I was really about to move into it. I started assessing what was needed. Suddenly, I felt overwhelmed. Even though it was just across the hall, the move seemed like a huge task.

I began by getting some sage and smudging the room completely, saying prayers of blessing for my new space. I asked for help, because my back hurt and I knew I couldn't do this move alone. For four mornings I smudged the room and gave thanks for what I was able to accomplish that day. After painting it and moving my furniture in, with the help of a friend, I felt much more centered. The last day, I moved my alter after making a place for it. Then I took my drum and sang a song that seemed to just come to me. Beating the drum from one room of the house to the other, visualizing the song gathering all of my energy together and depositing it into my new room, I said prayers of thanksgiving for my old room. As I sang, I found myself stopping the drumming in the center of my new space. As I looked around I could really feel myself expanding to fit the room.

When Annie told us that she would be moving, Inge and I had sat down and made a list of what we wanted: "Female, nondrinking, non-smoking, etc. . . ." Then I got out a bigger paper and made a list of all the qualities we wanted in the person: "Sense of humor, fun, enjoys communi-ty, independent yet likes to share meals once in a while, easygoing, spiri-tual orientation, not religious necessarily." Our second list was longer than the first. It was our wish list. It gave us time to talk about what we wanted and what we didn't want.

When we were finished, Inge took the small list and typed it up; I took it to the print shop and ran off some copies, which she took to various places around town where we would be most likely to find someone . . . like Sharon.

After meeting several prospective housemates, we met Sharon. We hit it off the first time—she loved the house and we seemed compatible. After lunch with her and a few more meetings, it was obvious to us that she was the one we were looking for. After she moved in, we decided to do a welcoming ritual.

A Rite of Welcoming

I had saved the water from Annie's rite, although at the time I wasn't sure exactly why. But when I began thinking about ways to wel-come Sharon into our house, I knew we could incorporate it somehow. It felt as though we were concluding the rite we started several weeks ear-lier—marking the transition the entire household was making.

Sharon was all moved in. We had found a time when we all could meet. We spoke briefly of ideas we had. Then we sat down around the same dining room table that we had used in Annie's moving rite. We had three candles, the bowl of water, some freshwater in a vase, and a yellow eggcup. I liked the idea of yellow as the color of the east, new beginnings.

Sharon wanted to talk a little about what we were each experienc-ing in our lives before we started. It seemed to me to be a good way to start the ritual.

After we finished sharing, I went over the ideas I had for the rite. They liked my plan and each of them contributed suggestions which we incorporated. Each of us lit a candle. I dipped the eggcup into the bowl of water left from Annie's rite and set it aside; then we took the bowl to the window and threw the old water out. Returning to the table, Sharon poured the freshwater into the bowl and Inge poured the water from the eggcup in also. I stirred it.

"Now we have freshwater which we can bless this house with, and bless ourselves. What is it we hope for in this new home?" I asked.

Sharon started, then Inge and me. When we finished I took some water and put it on the other women's heads and repeated what they had requested. I received a blessing from them, and they also blessed each other. When we finished, we sprinkled water around the dining room, saying words of blessing and sharing our hopes.

"We used to watch the priest do this during mass," Inge said. "The difference now is we're doing it for ourselves."

"That's quite a difference," I replied, smiling.

"I'm not completely comfortable with it. I wonder if it really works," Inge said honestly.

"It feels good to me to bless our home. Setting our intention for sharing our space is pretty important," Sharon commented.

"It seems to work for me," I said, grinning.

Creating Your Own Ritual

Of course your needs will vary, but setting the intention in the household is an important way to begin any living situation. In families it can help the children understand that they are an important part of the family, and can effectively improve the climate of the household, especially with teenagers.

My sister Sara sat down with her two young sons and created a family motto together, which they wrote out, framed, and placed over their kitchen table. They choose a home environment that is a safe, loving place, where everyone can talk about their feelings and share honestly with one another. When things get out of hand, their motto helps the family remember their agreed-upon intention. It helps to reestablish the connection they share and provides a touchstone of communication.

Here are suggestions for setting intention for the kind of home atmosphere you wish to cultivate:

1. Answer the following questions with your family or housemates: What do I want my home to be? How do I want it to feel?

To facilitate this, you can have a playful kitchen-table discussion that will help bring the members of your home together to make a list of agreed-upon qualities. If there are children, encourage them to write out and/or decorate the intention with crayons, pens, or craft supplies.

2. When you have compiled your list of desired qualities, you can create a simple rite of dedication by lighting a candle and hanging the finished product on the wall, officially proclaiming it to be a touchstone for your home. The intention may change and evolve with the needs of the household, and should not necessarily become etched in stone. If you or someone else needs it to change, rededicate!

3. Be sure to allow everyone to contribute to the rite as well as to the list of qualities. This is important in order for each person to feel part of what you are jointly creating.

26
Surgery and Life-Threatening Changes

The Friend

This one
leads you
inside,
a still pool
in deep forest.

Phil came to visit Thelma in the hospital the day before her surgery. An old friend, Phil was also Thelma's family physician. Although not a heart surgeon, he had agreed to scrub into surgery during the procedure. It was important to Thelma that Phil be there.

The next day as the nurse rolled her through the doors of the operating room, Thelma found herself becoming nervous and full of anxiety. Suddenly Phil appeared, leaning over her. "Hi, Thelma, how are you doing?" Phil's beaming face helped Thelma pour out her concern.

"I'm worried about this," she confessed. "I haven't felt nervous until now. I know this is a major procedure, that I might die. I want some reassurance that the staff will be respectful."

"Thelma, no one is going to say anything derogatory during your procedure. They are here to help you through this as much as anything. Bill Jennings is a wonderful man besides being a very fine surgeon. Why don't we talk to him now?" As Thelma entered the preoperative rooms, Phil spotted the surgeon.

"Bill, Thelma has some anxiety about the conversation among the staff during surgery. Can we discuss this together before we begin?" Phil sounded very at ease. Thelma felt better just knowing he was there. A few moments later Thelma was wheeled through the doors of the operating room as Phil talked to his colleague. The attending nurses and surgery staff were coming in to scrub. Then the two doctors came in, still conversing through their masks. Bill Jennings came over to Thelma and spoke to her kindly.

"Hi, Mrs. Bennett, I hear you're a little nervous about this procedure. Is there anything I can help you with, any questions you might have that I haven't answered clearly? I want you to feel at ease before we begin."

"Please call me Thelma. Doctor Jennings, I'm worried about what people will say while I'm under the knife. I don't want any jokes or negative talk or idle conversation. I need to have a reverent and positive approach," Thelma said honestly.

"We take any surgery very seriously, especially a major operation like heart surgery. I understand your anxiety, and your request is a good one; let me assure you that we will respect your wishes."

Then Thelma said suddenly, "Doctor, could we begin with a little prayer?" Dr. Jennings looked at Thelma over his mask. His eyes were wrinkled and looked kind. She hoped he was smiling beneath his mask. He nodded. "If it would make you feel better . . . I suppose it would help set the tone for the whole procedure. It's an unusual request, but I'm willing to if it helps you. Would you like to begin?" Thelma smiled and nodded affirmatively.

She closed her eyes and said, "Great Spirit, thank you for being in this room today. I know you are living through all of us, and we ask for the best results of this surgery. I ask that you guide the hands, thoughts, and hearts of these fine people to provide the best environment for my surgery. I pray for the best outcome possible. I ask that this prayer calm me. Help me to know that I'm in good hands. Amen."

Dr. Jennings looked at Thelma. "How are you feeling?"

"Better. Do you mind if I add something?"

"Go ahead, Thelma," he replied.

She continued. "I give thanks for all the helpful people here at this hospital, and I pray for anyone else facing surgery that they have the best possible results. I pray for all the doctors that they can be as receptive and open as these doctors and nurses. Thank you for guiding their skillful hands in this procedure. I pray for a good outcome. Amen."

Thelma felt at peace. She looked at Dr. Jennings and Phil.

Dr. Jennings said quietly, "Thelma, I want you to know that you will come through this with flying colors."

"Thank you, Doctors." She looked each of the staff around the table and said, "Thank you. I'm ready now; you can begin."

The next day Thelma woke up in the recovery room with Phil and her husband, Bob, on either side of her bed. She was unable to move but, after she became more lucid, she looked at her husband and said, "Bob, I had the best dream. I felt that there were angels all around me, that I was held in this cradle of love. It was wonderful."

She slowly turned her head and looked at Phil. "How did the surgery go?"

Phil smiled, "It went very well. I'll give you the details later. You are going to be just fine, Thelma!"

"Well, we asked for the best possible outcome, and it looks like that's what we got," Thelma said, smiling.

A few days after Thelma had been moved back to her room, Phil came to visit. He pulled out an article and laid it on the nightstand.

"Thelma, when you're up to it, I brought you this article. It's a study on the effects of prayer in a hospital in California. It says that it really makes a difference. I thought you might be interested. I made a copy for Bill Jennings, too. Read it when you're feeling better. I'm going to do the rest of my rounds. Good to see you awake and smiling."

Creating Your Own Ritual

There are many ways to do a ritual before surgery. Many procedures are done early in the morning, and the patient comes in a few hours before. It is for this reason that it may work best to do a ritual the night before, at home with family or friends.

To avoid any last-minute complications, it would be best to discuss any prayers like Thelma's with your doctor in advance. It is unusual to spontaneously create something like Thelma's ritual right in the operating room. Although Thelma had the advantage of having Phil for a friend, many doctors would not be opposed to pausing a moment before a procedure and saying a few words of blessing. But it is best to check ahead of time.

If the idea of prayer is uncomfortable to you, ask your higher power for what you need. Listen within for an answer. Perhaps you want a friend or loved one to bless you with flowers. They can touch your head and heart with a single blossom. Maybe there's a song you need to sing. I suggest you keep the ritual small and to the point. A simple prayer or request for help is all that's needed. Elaborate rites won't work in busy, crowded hospital rooms.

Consider inviting friends and family to your home the night before to pray for the best outcome. You may want to pass a talking stick as a way to share feelings openly (see chapter 15). You should probably include only those who will help you relax and stay calm.

Be sure to ask for support from friends and the nursing staff. You may find that what you asked for in your ritual comes through them. If you have a lot of fear about being in a hospital, you might want to let someone on staff know so you can talk to the chaplain or a counselor. Hospital staffs are full of caring people; allow yourself to be cared for, and ask for what you need. Also be aware that many hospital personnel are very busy and overworked. It is important to ask questions, monitor your own medication as a double-check, and be vigilant about your own postoperative care. It maybe very helpful to have a family member act as an advocate for you if you are too sick.

Another Way to Create Your Own Ritual

Here is another rite you can do before surgery if you know of the procedure in advance. It can support you or your loved ones with the strength they need at home before and after the procedure.

Have the person facing surgery sit in the center of a circle with unlit votive candles all around her or him. Each person attending the ritual brings with them something symbolizing a quality—such as patience (for example, a stone can represent the gift of patience), healing (a scarf blessed by friends and family may represent healing), or strength—that helped them through a tough time. You can also pass a stone and have each person put their quality in it, so the patient can take it along to the hospital.

When everyone has joined the circle, each person gives their gift to the person in the center, telling the story of the object and/or a story from their life describing their ordeal. They can begin with the words "I give you the gift of . . ." The person in the center, receiving the gift, says, "I accept the gift of patience (strength, healing, et cetera) from you and give you light." The person then lights a candle and hands it to whoever just gave the gift. The rite continues in this manner until everyone has had a turn.

When the rite is over, the person in the center is surrounded by friends with their candles. You can blow the candles out or let them burn down. The candles could also be taken home by the participants to be lit on the day of the procedure, to focus energy or pray for the person having surgery. Group hugs are often a great way to end any rite.

27

Ceremony
for Lost Body Parts

I'm taking this moment . . .

to open to a darker sun,
to weep
to feel
all that is unspoken.
Laughing, holding hands
everything left undone,

Autumn leaves tossed
by winter winds.

Beverly had just gone through a mastectomy. She felt great grief from loosing her breast. Her support group, lead by her therapist, helped a lot. Many of them were women recovering from breast surgery themselves.

One night her therapist, Jean, suggested they hold a memorial service for the loss of her breast at the next session. It would be a time for all of them to grieve their own losses. Each had a different cancer diagnosis and was recovering from a different procedure. Jean suggested that all the women make a facsimile of their missing body part from clay or modeling wax, or by drawing or painting whatever they had lost. Beverly was to bring hers to the next meeting.

The night of the ritual Beverly and the other women cleared the space in the room so they could make a circle. The five women sat together around a scarf they used as an altar cloth. In the center they placed a candle and some water in a bowl.

In addition to the drawings Beverly made of her surgery process and her missing breast, each of the other women brought a meaningful object signifying strength. Some brought their work-in-progress to share with the rest of the group. Beverly laid several drawings around the candle. One of her pictures showed how she wanted to feel about herself even without her breast; in that picture she was one-breasted and jumping for joy, surrounded by yellow and pink light. She also brought photographs of her husband and family and friends.

After each woman told about the object she had brought, Jean began by taking the bowl of water and sprinkling it around the room to bless the space. Then she asked Beverly to focus on the drawing she had made of her missing breast. As Beverly looked at her drawing, Jean suggested that she invite the spirit of her missing breast to enter the room.

Beverly closed her eyes and took several slow, deep breaths. When she opened them again she began to talk to the picture about her feelings. Her eyes were steady and clear. She shared her sadness and her grief. She thanked her breast for being a part of her and told it how much she missed it. She thanked it for serving her, for feeding her children, for providing pleasure for herself and her husband. She apologized for not appreciating it more while she had it. She thanked it for the sacrifice it had made so that she could go on living. She closed her eyes and visualized the picture in her mind's eye.

Then her therapist suggested softly, "Beverly, ask it if it has anything to share with you—that it wants you to know."

Beverly's eyes were close tightly, tears streaming out of the corners. She took a deep breath. After a while she began to smile slightly.

"What did it say?" Jean inquired.

"It said, I love you too. Bless me and let me go; you have the gift of life," Beverly replied quietly. She sat for a while feeling sad, and fortunate to be alive. Then she asked Jean to take a handful of water from the bowl and anoint her chest.

Jean was surprised and honored to be asked. She took the water and, touching Beverly where her breast had been, said, "I bless you, Beverly. You have been given the gift of life. You, Beverly, are whole and alive!" At that she dipped her hand in the water and sprinkled it over Beverly, touching her head and her heart.

As the ritual ended, each woman asked to have a night in the center of the circle to talk to the spirit of what they had lost. Jean agreed that this would be important, so as not to take away from Beverly's experience and to support each member in her own grieving process.

As they concluded, Beverly said, "I think I need to let my pictures go in some reverent way, like burning them or burying them, releasing them to spirit." Jean supported her by saying that it was an important aspect of her healing to release the breast she had lost. Letting go would help her to accept herself as she is now. Jean encouraged the other women to do the same. Most decided to wait until their rite in future meetings.

At the end of the evening, the women joined hands and said a prayer of thanksgiving. As they were ready to leave, Beverly gave Jean a hug and whispered, "Thank you."

Creating Your Own Ritual

Everyone's experience with surgery and recovery is different, even though the procedure may be similar. Support groups can be of great help, especially if the diagnosis is cancer. Most hospitals have cancer support groups as part of their outpatient services. If support groups are not available in your area, I recommend you start one with a supportive group of friends and a therapist who is trained in leading groups.

You can begin your rite for surgery in stages: before the procedure, following surgery, and during recovery. Before surgery, sit with a friend, your therapist, or a companion and light a candle to help center yourself. Place your hand over your body part. Breath into your hand, then speak to the part you are about to lose. Listen, and take time to hear an answer. Say good-bye and let yourself grieve.

For the ritual after surgery, any art material can be used for the facsimile. You can use clay and then release the unfired clay figure into a stream. You can use papier-mâché, paint it, and then burn it to let go of the spirit of the missing part. Read over Beverly's rite again for helpful suggestions. Let your intuition and imagination be your guide.

SECTION FOUR

HONORING
RELATIONSHIPS

28
A New Relationship

Egret Wings

Like a striding egret in green moss,
or the gentle lifting of her wings
or her delicate lancing of earth for food,
therein lies the reason that I love.

Tom and I were visiting friends at a farm they had just bought south of Humboldt, California, near the coast. We took off by ourselves for the first day and headed to the beach.

This beach was different from the other beaches. It was a black-sand beach, which occurs rarely in California, and had unusual cliffs with green copper creeks coming out of the rocks.

We explored, walked, and played on the beach for a long way. It was a weekday, so there weren't many other people. After a long walk we came to some rocks that rose right out of the sand. They were huge out-croppings extending from the cliffs.

"This looks like a good place to sit and rest," Tom said.

We flopped onto the sand using the sloping rocks as a back rest. After a while we began talking again.

"This is just perfect." I said grinning.

"Yea, a good place for a ritual." Tom looked at me with one eye and smiled.

"I guess we could use one. What are you thinking?" I asked.

"Well I don't know exactly, but I think we need something to af-firm our new entwining lives together. Something to admit that we are a unit." We had just finished talking about what commitment meant to us.

"That's a great idea." I replied. As we spoke I could see us making a mandala or a large round picture in the sand near the water. Mandalas are used in meditation in some eastern religions.

"What if we made a mandala together? We could start with a circle, and see where it goes." I said sitting up ready to go.

"Draw, I don't know ..." Tom said hesitantly.

"Come on I'll show you it will be easy, we'll just play with it."

With that reassurance Tom popped up and we walked out on the sand that glistened in the late afternoon sun.

We stood on opposite side of each other on a large expanse of beach. I grabbed a long stick of driftwood, Tom found a dried stick of bull-whip kelp. I put my stick in the sand and started to inscribe a very large circle.

"Let's give ourselves lots of room," I said, laughing. I think we are making a mandala. Perhaps a big "C."

Tom smiled. "Oh, the 'C' word again!" (C for commitment), he said playfully, having just finished a discussion about our fears of commitment.

He started at the opposite side and began drawing the circle from his side. When our lines met and we were standing roughly where the other had started, we moved into the center of the circle. Each of our designs and directions was unique. We began to play with the form inside. Sometimes our lines crossed and sometimes they merged. We played with our tracks in the sand as well as the patterns our sticks made.

Then without saying a word we expanded beyond the circle. Tom began spinning like a shot-putter and then launched his stick. It flew over the mandala and landed on the other side, casting a long, squiggly shadow in the waning sunlight.

I paused for a moment and looked at him. It seemed like he was actually launching himself into outer space. His actions blended with our ideas about relationships. We wanted ours to be a container for our unlimited growth and exploration of ourselves, each other, and the universe. Could I accept the challenge he had just put before me? I wound my arm up like a baseball pitcher, then I spun in place, and with one last spin of my arm, let go of my stick.

We stood for a long time, looking at our creation. My stick had landed not far from his. Their shadows made unique lines in the sand.

"So, this is what our life together will look like in fifty years?" I said, cocking my head to look up at him.

He smiled and replied, "I think it will be even more interesting than we could imagine."

We gathered our things and headed back to our car, arm in arm. As we walked down the beach, it seemed as though the ritual had helped us take one more step closer together.

Creating Your Own Ritual

If you are in a committed relationship, rites can help you make the adjustments as you move closer together. This rite, along many others, helped Tom and I take the small steps to acknowledge the changes that occurred in our life since we fell in love.

How you create such rites for yourself is very personal. They come naturally out of your developing intimacy. They can be fun, too. Talk it over with your beloved. See what might work for you. You don't need a beach to create a rite—just the willingness to embrace the next step.

29
Friendship Changes

You Know Me

I will always know you
through this bond we share,
by this infinitely rich river
of golden moonlight.

Jesse and I stopped at the coffee shop to get a cup of tea before the movie. The last time we saw a movie together was before I met Tom. The months had flown by. After several years of being single women together, our lives had suddenly taken very different paths. We used to see each other every week; now it was once a month, although we spoke on the phone frequently. She was one of my dearest friends, and I wanted to tell her the news in person. After we had gotten our drinks and sat down, I looked at her, and we smiled at each other.

"Well how are you, Robin? It's so good to see you. How are things going with Tom?" Jesse had reached her hand across the small table as she talked. I grasped it and we sat there for a moment.

"I'm feeling great. Tom and I are well. He's such a wonderful man." I took a deep breath. Jesse's face beamed with the love of a friend. "Jesse, I have something to tell you." I drew another deep breath. "We're engaged," I said with a smile. "We head to Santa Barbara this week so I can meet his family."

Jesse sat back in her chair and put her hands to her mouth in one movement as she gasped, "Oh, Robin, I am so happy for you! I know you waited a long time for the right one." Her hands dropped as she spoke, and her beaming face clouded over. I asked her what was wrong. This time I reached for her hand.

"Oh, you know, relationship changes, the inevitable. I miss you, Rob. I really miss you." Jesse had a catch in her voice.

"I miss you too, Jess."

"We haven't talked in so long," she continued. "Would you mind if we didn't go to the movie tonight? I just want to catch up."

In a few minutes we were in Jesse's apartment. She lit a candle and made us some fresh tea. Then we sat down together.

"Jess, I hate this part of women's relationships. I don't want to be the one who dumps my friends when I find a man. It's happened to me and it hurts. I feel really uncomfortable; I feel like I've done that with you, even though we've talked on the phone. I'm so sorry, I don't know how to make this shift easily."

"It's inevitable, and you have stayed in touch, but we spent so much more time together than we have recently."

Jesse was right; we had both been busy. We had gone to concerts and movies—something almost every week. We recalled some of the times we spent together. I missed our friendship too.

"The funny thing is," Jesse continued, "I still feel we are close friends; I just don't see you as much." She sat back in her chair, smiling at me with sad eyes.

"I know, I feel like Tom and I have been nurturing this newborn relationship. It has felt so new and tender. I've barely been able to talk to anyone about the changes inside and the growth we've both done. It's been phenomenal. I'm not the woman you knew even a month ago."

"I can see it—you just glow." Jesse smiled, then her face grew sad and she looked down at her hands. "That's the hardest part for me. When I talk to you I feel sad. You remind me of all the things in my life I want and don't have. Then I feel guilty because I love you and I want to stay in touch. I would love to find someone. At my age it doesn't seem likely. I'm so tired of being alone, and I am so afraid to love someone again."

"Listen girlfriend, if you really want to find someone, they'll show up—I don't care how old you are. You're just in your fifties. I know women in their seventies and eighties who have found someone to love and been very happy."

"I know, that's the problem—just looking at the possibility, I see all the baggage I have. I feel overwhelmed and hopeless."

For a long time we spoke about the changes relationships require, what you have to let go of, and the fears—of remarrying; of getting hurt again, of loosing oneself. I told her Tom wasn't like the others. We both had had fear to work through. Getting back to the love between us was a real challenge that took a lot of time and attention. It was definitely worth it, especially because we were laying the foundation for the rest of our lives.

"Robin, I'm sorry to lay all this on you; here you're getting married and I'm all doom and gloom."

152

"No, Jesse, between you and me something big has shifted. I think it's important to acknowledge that. You're right, we used to spend a lot of time together—I miss that. It's only recently that I feel as though I can see friends again and reestablish connections with people."

"I feel the love between us, as always, Robin. We have shared so much and I'm so grateful."

"I feel like I want to acknowledge with a little ritual this change we have gone through together. Just now, I'm seeing this figure eight of fire looping around us, affirming the love between us that never dies. Does that feel all right with you?"

"Yes, and I have a special candle I want to use."

Jesse got up from the table and went into the bedroom. When she returned she had a large ball-shaped candle in her hands. "I love this candle. I keep it on my altar. It's the circle of change, of everything continuous."

Jesse lit the candle, and we stood facing each other, the candle glowing between us. "Show me what you had in mind, Rob."

Without saying a word I took the candle in my left hand and slowly passed it around Jesse; I had to step forward and we fell into a warm hug. As I took the candle in my right hand we slowly let go, and I stepped back, bringing the candle between us. Our four hands rested around the glowing ball.

"We make a medicine wheel with our thumbs," I said, surprised.

"Yes, a Celtic cross," Jesse added.

We smiled warmly at each other, and then she took the candle. She passed it around me and stepped forward, embracing for a long moment. Then she brought it back to the center. Again our four hands held it between us. We stood in silence for a moment longer. When I looked up at my dear friend, the candle flickered, lighting her loving face. The sadness was gone. Then she whispered, "I feel really clean, really complete, and so much better. I love you, Robin."

"And I love you, Jesse." We stood for a moment longer.

"Ready?" I asked. She nodded. "May the flame of our love continue always. One, Two, Three!"

Together we bent over and blew the candle out.

Creating Your Own Ritual

One of the biggest conflicts women often have is when an intimate relationship forms outside the friendship. It is difficult to make these transitions, but this ritual helped me and my friend. It is important to note that before the ritual could take place, we had to take the time to process our feelings about the changes. That wasn't easy, but it was critical to our friendship continuing. It also laid the groundwork for a successful rite.

There are many ways a friendship can change. Moving disrupts relationships; so does changing jobs or even starting in a new position at work. Divorce is another way relationships change, and so is starting classes, or ending them.

If you want to create a rite like this, first talk to your friend; share this story with him or her. Then find a candle that suits you—any one will do.

30
A Unique Wedding

Heart Color

Inside your heart,
I am surprised to see
my rose color painted.

It wasn't what their friends or family expected: spending the weekend at a secluded hot springs resort in the hills of California with people they didn't know. But Cloe and Randy didn't care about having a typical wedding. They were interested in a meaningful one. They wanted to bring their families and friends together, to give them time to get to know one another, and give everyone a relaxing time in one place. They wanted to take each aspect of their wedding ceremony in stages, step by step.

"I can't take a whole weekend off for you guys to get married; why don't you do it in an afternoon like everyone else?" Cloe's friend Jo Ellen hissed at them.

"You've got to be kidding! I'm suppose to drive there and spend the weekend? Can't I just drop by for the ceremony? What time does it start?" her brother asked.

"It's not in a place where you can just drop by. That's why we have rented the whole resort for the weekend. And we consider the whole event—Friday evening until Sunday morning—the ceremony. So we're asking everyone to come for the weekend or don't come." Cloe hung up the phone.

"I can't believe these responses," she fumed. "Why are they so resistant to enjoying themselves for the weekend?"

"Cloe, this is our wedding," Randy said, "We know what we want. If they want to come, fine; if not, then we'll do it with those who want to be there. That's enough for me. I think people are resistant to anything new or different. We just have to be strong in what we want and stick to it."

One by one their friends and family responded to the wedding invitation. To Randy and Cloe's surprise, most every one decided to come.

Friday night everyone gathered at Wilbur Hot Springs, near

Williams, California. Tucked back in the hills several miles off a dirt road, it is a quiet place, just right for a secluded weekend. That night after supper Randy shared his thoughts about the event with everyone: "We wanted to take this weekend step by step. We want you folks to walk with us through this very important time in our lives. Those of you here have meant the most to us."

When he was done speaking, Cloe said, "Tonight we want to take time to honor our guests who have come so far for this event. Each of you is significant to us." The two of them took turns speaking to their guests, recognizing the importance of each one.

The next morning after breakfast they had time to share the meaning of their vows. They wanted everyone to understand what they were witnessing. Cloe explained, "We are committing to each other day by day. We see every day as a new opportunity for commitment and growth."

Then Randy added, "That doesn't mean we won't be married for a lifetime; we just want to see our life together as a dynamic process, not a setup for stagnation." They went through the meaning of each one of their vows and answered questions. "We'll have the ceremony before dinner tonight at five o'clock," Randy added. "Then a farewell Sunday brunch tomorrow. The rest of the time is your own; there are trails here and of course the hot tubs and swimming pool. Enjoy yourselves."

That night at five the guests gathered in the main room of the lodge. It was decorated with roses and ribbons. The service was officiated by a friend, and various members of the wedding party sang songs and recited poems. When the service was over they gathered around the table and shared a delicious dinner prepared by the resort staff with the help of some friends. After they cut the cake, Randy announced, "We have a surprise. We're going to have a little concert by Jake and Eileen, who are professional musicians. They're giving us the concert as a wedding gift."

The next day Randy and Cloe enjoyed the day with their friends and families. Everyone commented on what a good time they had had.

"Let's do this every year," one guest said.

Another one added, "I've never been to such a beautiful wedding. I love the way everyone is so relaxed and calm. It's because we took the time to enjoy the event and each other."

Cloe and Randy were glad they stuck to their deepest desire and followed their hearts.

Creating Your Own Ritual

I offer this wedding rite to illustrate that if you do something out of the ordinary, you may run into some resistance. However, this is the time when your clarity of intention, courage, and strength of purpose are tested. Sometimes it takes a little heat to weld one's resolve.

Everyone has a different style to their wedding. This one was unusual not only because of the weekend-long commitment by the guests and the different stages, but also because it was calm and relaxed—the antithesis of some of the frantic events I have attended.

I also offer this ceremony as a way to show how we can ease the tension of such a major event and make things more pleasant for ourselves as well as our guests. Spending more time with one another helps the parties get to know each other better. Of course you can do the same in a block of rooms at a hotel. However, the seclusion of a resort helps contain the event differently and prevents people from just dropping by.

One thing to ask yourself is: What do I really want for my wedding? Start a list. A great book for helping you plan your wedding in detail is: *Weddings from the Heart* by Daphne Rose Kingma.*25 It gives great tips for planning a uniquely personal wedding, from what and whom to include to writing your own vows.

31
Honoring the Mother of the Bride

New Paths

I toss rose petals
to bless you on your way.

Now I turn slowly
to take the first steps
on my new and invisible path,
stretching out,
blossoming green,
      uncharted.

W hen I arrived at Dora's house she was already in her robe. "Let's set
the table up in my daughter's bedroom," she said. "It's symbolic to me,
letting go of her and shedding the wedding responsibilities. Besides," she
chuckled, "all the presents are in my room."

I followed her upstairs to her daughter's room. The walls were covered with childhood memorabilia, including drawings of horses, ribbons
from competitions, and pictures of movie stars.

"My daughter's wedding was a full-time job for me for the last
several months—so many details. Now I feel the impact, like I'm shat-
tered inside. I know you can help me heal again. I'm completely open to
any suggestions you may have that will help."

I set up my massage table and drew the blinds while Dora told me
about the wedding, how beautiful her daughter looked and how happy she
was with her new husband.

"As I sat there listening to their vows, I realized I took care of every detail for the wedding. It could not have been more perfect. The only
imperfection was me: I didn't get my hair or nails done—I didn't even get
a dress I particularly liked. Everything else went off without a hitch. But I
felt like a mess."

"Well, I'm glad you called," I said. "This is the beginning of your
time now. I'll leave the room so you can get onto the table."

When I returned to the room, I straightened the sheet and made her more comfortable with cushions and soft music. Over the next hour I firmly and gently kneaded the stiffness out of her body. As I finished I held her feet and said a little prayer for her recovery, and I imagined her in a cocoon of pink and golden light. When I was through I left the room so she could really rest. Later I returned to help her back into her robe.

"I feel so much better, really cleaned out and mended. Thank you, Robin."

"Dora, you may need to include this as part of an ongoing transition for yourself for the next few weeks."

"Oh, yes," she replied. "Today marks the beginning of a major turning point for me. This morning I finished a letter to my daughter to be read on her honeymoon. I needed to share with her some things I wish my mother had shared with me. I wanted to honor her independence and life direction. I'm so proud of her."

"What else are you doing for you, Dora?"

She explained that she was spending a lot of time keeping a journal. Her dreams and intuition were telling her that she needed some time alone.

"I'm taking a few days this week to spend at my friend's cabin. My husband will join me on Friday; he needs some time to rest, too."

She told me that she needed to be alone to help close the child-rearing chapter of her life and open a new one. The new chapter is about developing her own interests and some new life directions. "Tonight a group of friends are taking me out to dinner. They are going to help me celebrate . . . and probably grieve a little."

We spoke of the significance of a wedding event for the parents. She stated that it is as big a transition for them as it is for the child getting married. "No one ever told me what a big impact it would have," Dora said wistfully. "It is the end of parenting. There isn't another thing I need to do to set her on her way."

"There is one more thing, Dora," I said. "And you are already doing it. You're modeling how to take good care of yourself. That's as important for her as it is for you. You love yourself enough to give yourself the time you need to recover and feel your own transformation. That is a great gift to your entire family."

Creating Your Own Transition

For the mother of the bride it can be fun and exhausting to help create a wedding for a daughter, but it's important to remember that a wedding is a family transition. It is a declaration of a shift in relationships that goes beyond the couple getting married. As a rite of passage for you, it may be enough for you to attend the wedding; however, whether you are the mother of the bride or of the groom, be sure to take some time for reflection.

Ask yourself: What is it that I really need now that the wedding is over? Make a list. Then ask yourself: How do I really feel? You may want to write in a journal your true feelings—about the wedding, your new life, your new son- or daughter-in-law . . . You need not share it with anyone—just express it; that is enough.

Take your list of needs and meet them. If you set your intention to include each item on your list as part of a rite, anything can become part of your transition ritual. Here are some suggestions that can help you create a rite of transition for yourself: get a massage or get your hair or nails done, and let your massage therapist, hairdresser, or manicurist know that you are recovering from your child's wedding; they can be more supportive during your appointment. Spend a few days alone or with your husband or a friend; set your intention to celebrate a new beginning with a special dinner with your husband or friend.

Here are some suggestions for creating a rite that helps you acknowledge all your feelings and gives you a way to set your new life path:

Ask your husband or one or more friends to witness your rite. You may also want to include your husband or partner. When you begin remember that rites are like stories, they have a beginning, a middle, and an end. You could start by drawing a circle of love around you, symbolized by dried rose petals or burning sage or incense.

Your rite can incorporate journal entries, a letter to your child to be read aloud, or a letter to God or your higher power about what you are learning as a part of the transition. You can also include several items on your list of needs. State what you want for the next phase of your life. This may include career directions, new experiences, or places in your inner self you have yet to discover. Ask your friends for help; you may want to ask for a foot rub or head massage as a part.

Close your rite by touching your heart and head with a rosewater, blessing yourself; or ask a friend or your husband to do this for you. You can also take turns blessing one another.

Above all, give yourself some time. Any major transition requires time to recovery. Big changes always imply loss, even when woven into the most joyful events. When you give yourself time to feel the transition, you help yourself take the first steps on your new life path.

160

32
Acknowledging Divorce

Pulled Threads

Perhaps
we were never the one
we dreamed.

Yesterday is a memory of
long ragged days
stitched together
and threads left
from mismatched seams

and the undoing.

Finding myself alone after eight years of marriage was quite a surprise. After a period of ignoring my feelings, I finally had to face the fact that if I wanted to be free of my anger and not carry the resentment into other relationships, I better get some help.

Brenda was a friend and a psychotherapist. I had been working with her for about a year, trying to clean up aspects of my past. With her guidance I felt freed from the pain and shame of failing to make my marriage work. I could let go with the realization that we simply weren't meant to be together anymore.

On the way home from a particularly helpful session one day, I felt the need for some sort of ritual closing of my married life. I stopped to purchase a few things to help me. I bought a length of rope and a candle. After arriving home I found an old piece of plywood out by the woodpile, and the ax we used to split firewood. I carried them to the back of the house along with the rope, candle, and a cushion.

Brown's Lake came up to the backyard behind the house. Sitting down on the earth, facing the lake and the setting sun, I placed the woodblock in front of me. Then I put the ax on the block with the rope. I rested the candle and matches at my side.

First I closed my eyes and imagined a circle of golden light around me. Doing so gave me a sense of protection and peace. I let it fill the space around my body about four feet in each direction. When I was ready to begin I tied one end of the rope to a heavy wood chair and held the other end in my left hand. With my right hand I picked up the ax and declared,

"Jason [my former spouse], I hereby sever my connections with you once and for all. I release any remaining anger, sadness, or feelings of resentment. I forgive you and I bless you and let you go on your journey. May you find peace." At that I let fall the ax and severe the rope.

Then I said, "Great Spirit, I forgive myself. I pray to find the mate who will support me as I support him, who accepts me for who I am and whom I can accept, someone I can grow with instead of against—all in the right timing. I light this candle as a symbol of my faith. I ask for blessings for this relationship yet to come. Thank you Father-Mother God."

I sat for a long time facing the setting sun, watching it go down over the trees. I felt shifts within myself as though I had cut some invisible cords that were now unraveling. I felt free, peaceful, and calm, knowing that the sun always rises in the morning.

Of course my way is not the only way. It all depends on the circumstances. The following story gives another approach to creating a personal rite of divorce.

A Second Ritual of Divorce

Peter and Jane had been able to remain friends through the entire ordeal of their divorce. They had a rare relationship, and they wanted their friendship to remain intact. This was important to both of them, partially because of the children they shared, but also because they truly cared about each other, even though they no longer wanted to be married any longer. They wanted to affirm their friendship and let go of the attachment and negativity of their marriage.

Their marriage counselor suggested they each make a list of the qualities of their relationship they wanted to keep intact. Then they noted what was the same on their lists, and looked together at the strain in their relationship. After discussing their individual lists they made three new lists together: what they wanted to keep, what they wanted to let go of, and what needed work.

After their session they stopped in the park to complete a conversation they had started in the counselor's office. What they had written down on the lists felt good to both of them. It was as though they were beginning a new phase of their relationship and had broken through blocks in communicating. They were gaining greater clarity to the ways they were relating that were positive and which they wanted to continue after the divorce.

They agreed to mark this new beginning with a celebration, so later that week they met for dinner. Afterward they walked to a nearby baseball field where they had spent a lot of time together with their youngest son. During their marriage they often joked that they spent more time there than at home. They had also spoken together philosophically about baseball being a metaphor for the game of life. The field held meaning for both of them.

When they arrived the field was empty. Peter retrieved a bag of practice baseballs out of the car. He was the coach of his son's Little League team. They walked together to the pitcher's mound. He placed the bag of balls, a couple of bats, and a crate in the center of the mound. Jane took one of the bats and drew a circle in the dirt around the two of them, where a chalk line was worn and almost invisible. Peter handed a ball to Jane. With chalk she wrote on the ball an aspect of their relationship they had agreed to release. As she read it out loud—"blaming each other"—she tossed it in the air and Peter hit it into the batter's fence. Jane took her turns hitting the ball while Peter wrote.

When they had completed the process, they gathered the balls scattered over home plate. They returned to the circle and Jane emptied the balls into the crate. Then she picked up one and wrote "support each other in decisions with the children," and handed the ball to Peter. Peter placed it in the bag. Then he took a ball and wrote, "We agree to speak positively to the children about the other parent." He handed the ball to Jane, and she popped it in the bag. Then she took another ball and wrote, "We agree to foster our friendship." She handed it to Peter, and he placed it in the bag.

When they had finished all the qualities they wanted to keep in their relationship, the two of them sat together with the bag of positive qualities between them. Peter made a joke about never making to first base with Jane again, and she responded with a joke about how that afternoon they had really batted a home run together. They agreed that if they could have this much fun sorting issues that remained between them, they would do quite well in the future working through any difficulties with the children.

When they were ready to go Jane and Peter opened the circle by rubbing out the line around the pitcher's mound. Then they hugged each other and walked to the car, arranging the next week's schedule for the children.

Creating Your Own Ritual

Not all relationships are as compatible after divorce as Peter and Jane's. However, keep in mind they did not work out everything they had at issue. They were taking time to celebrate the breakthrough they had made together in the counselor's office and letting go of what they could. The two rituals are offered as ideas you might find helpful in formulating your own ritual for divorce.

You may find that your ex-spouse is not willing to participate in anything you would want to create. It is not necessary to have both partners present. Doing a ritual for yourself, as I did, can be very effective, and all you may need do.

Before you start here are some questions you may ask yourself when considering this ritual:

1) Do I want to completely sever my relationship with my former spouse?

2) If so, are there other relationships effected by the divorce that I want to maintain (for example, mutual friends, the spouse's parents, siblings, children, or other relatives)? How will severing this relationship effect those relationships?

3) If not, in what ways and for what reasons do I want to remain connected?

4) Is it desirable to do a ritual of divorce together?

5) Should we include the children? Including the children is not recommended if they are too young to understand what is happening. On the other hand, children understand symbols more clearly than conceptual language. If they are included it could also be a way for them to express their feelings about the divorce. I recommend that you consult your counselor, minister, rabbi, or therapist for input. Ask the children if they want to participate, and let them know clearly what you are getting them into.

6) What are the aspects of this relationship that I want to let go of?

7) What are the aspects that I want to keep?

8) How have I changed as a result of sharing my life with this person? Positively? Negatively?

9) What new areas of my life can I claim as I look forward to life as a single adult?

10) What am I afraid of?

Designing the Ritual Format

Here are some questions to help you form a ritual for releasing friendships or lover relationships that no longer feel healthy, as well as a past marriage. It is most helpful to consider these questions after answering the ones above.

1) Who, if anyone, would I/we like to include in this rite?
2) What objects would I/we want to include?
3) Where should it take place?
4) How should I/we begin it?
5) What will be the focal point of the rite?
6) What do I/we need to do to complete this relationship as symbolized in the rite?
7) What do I want to maintain in the relationship?
8) How can I incorporate 'letting go' with the aspects of the relationship that I want to maintain?
9) How will the ritual close?

33
Two Funerals

Last Moments

She sleeps, restlessly,
occasionally wincing with pain.
Her eyes open when she hears my creaking step.
Her spider-hand reaches for me.
I hold it gently and stroke her paper skin.
As she falls to sleep again
I watch the years of difference
folded between our fingers.

She is my grandmother, the toughest one I know.
Now she lay, life ebbing,
and I can only hold her hand.

I cradle her like a frail hatchling.
It's time,
and I stay for a while,
drawing circles on her palm.

The phone rang. As I heard my mother's voice, I sat down on the bed slowly, knowing that this was the call I was dreading. Grandma had died less than an hour before.

"This is the end of an era, Mom," I said through the lump in my throat.

"I know, honey, your grandma was something else. I wish you could come home, Robin."

"I know, Mom, I wish I could, too. But I just can't be in two places at one time." Both my parents were understanding of my situation. I had just returned to California after being with the family in Rockford, Illinois, for more than a month during semester break from graduate school. Since I could not afford make a second trip home nor miss classes, I could not return for the funeral.

We all felt that it was more important for me to be with Grandma while she was alive than after she was gone. I had spent many hours with her and shared some very special moments during my stay. I said good-bye for the last time on my way to the airport, one week before my mother's call.

"You do what you need to, honey. Your Dad will send you a tape of the service." We cried for a while before she had to phone the rest of my family. Mom had given me the date and time of the memorial service. I had been thinking about a way to say good-bye to Grandma from California; I would hold my own service at the same time.

After the call I went upstairs to my friend Mary Ellen's room; we lived in the dormitory. I knew she was a person with whom I could cry. We talked and sobbed and shared memories of friends and family whom we had lost. I asked her if she would help me create a memorial service. She was delighted and became the organizer. She selected the music and coordinated others whom I asked to attend.

While Mary Ellen and I conferred about plans, my family in Rockford, with the help of Pastor Jim Roberts from Emmanuel Lutheran Church (our childhood parish), organized a service to be held in the chapel of the retirement home where my grandma spent the last few months of her life. On February 6, we held two services for her—one in Rockford, Illinois, and one in Alameda, California.

The service in Rockford, led by Pastor Roberts started with a prayer, followed by Psalm 121: "My help cometh from the hills from whence I came . . ." He mentioned that several family members could not be there but acknowledged that we were present in spirit. He started by reading a letter from my sister Sara who lived in Denver, which she wrote to Grandma after a recent holiday visit:

Dear Grandma,

I wanted to write you a letter to let you know all the things I didn't get to say to you when I was home. . . . I've always admired your feisty independence. You have been a wonderful role model for me. Your strength and character have been especially meaningful for me since I have been on my own. It has been hard to depend only on myself.

You have always made us feel proud of our heritage. I liked talking about where our names came from, or where this or that came from. Its a very warm stabilizing feeling to know you have roots when life is trying to blow you over. . . . You represent our link to all of that.

I know we had a very rich childhood, and you were a big part of it and continue to be as we have grown and raise our kids. They are lucky to have a great-grandma like you. I love you very much. Thanks for giving me the tradition and love and strength that is so helpful to me today. I'll call you soon.

Sara

At the same time in California, my friends and I gathered at the bird sanctuary in Alameda, a few miles from school.

"She would have loved this place," I said to my friends. Grandma loved birds and wild animals. I watched herons and egrets and other marsh birds live and play right under the planes that took off from Oakland Airport.

My friends didn't know Grandma, but they knew me. The gathering consisted of myself and Mary Ellen; a Catholic priest from Ireland named Daniel; Jeff, a Methodist minister from Illinois; his wife, Therese; their daughter, Margaret; and several others who were dear to me. We opened the service standing in a circle on the beach. We lit sage to cleanse the air and ourselves. I asked my friend Jeff to do some drumming. Mary Ellen and other friends helped to weave a nice rhythm between songs, poems, and stories.

Next Mary Ellen sang "Eagle's Wings." Her voice and the song helped me see my grandma's spirit soar with the birds. I knew that my brother-in-law Ralph would lead my family in the same song in Rockford. Through the melody, and the image of my grandmother's spirit soaring with the eagles, I felt connected to my relatives.

I asked Daniel to read the story I wrote about Grandma. Pastor Roberts read the same story in Illinois:

Lake Ripples

At the bottom of my heart is a lake, deep and blue. Through the shallow edges of the lake one can see rocks move and change against the sandy bottom. As I watch the rocks, one rises from the bottom, a long periscope head cruises atop the water, looking at me with indifference. The turtle speaks:

"Your grandmother sends a ripple across this lake which I call home. When I dive again she will be released to the spirit world. Before your heart will let her spirit fly, is there anything you wish to say to her before I dive again?"

My mind stirred at the edge of the lake. "Turtle, please, help me to honor her. I want her to know she has been important to all of us; I want her to know that I love her. You who first carried the earth from the bottom of the sea, help me in honoring my grandmother."

Turtle paddled around the cool blue water as though pacing the floor, searching for a response to my request. After a time it paddled straight to me and looked into my eyes.

"Child, you honor your grandmother every day in the way you carry her unseen gifts with you. She has given you dignity, and you hold your head high. She has given you grace, and you walk as the heron moves through the water. She has shown you perseverance, and you too complete your tasks with steadfastness. She has given you strength, and you show that strength in the way you bravely change course with each new choice you make. She has given you wisdom by sharing her life with you, telling you of her hardships as well as her joys, so that you might not have the same difficulties. She has given you love. As you love others, remember how well she loved you. You, my child, must know that as you walk the earth with your grandmother's gifts, you honor her. Know this and know also that her gifts live in you and in your children.

As Turtle finished speaking, I offered Turtle some snails that I collected as a gift of thanks. As Turtle reached for them, the snails fell free and sank into the water like stones. Turtle dove after them. My grandmother crossed into the spirit world.

I sat at the edge of the lake for a long time until the sun turned orange and the sky purple. The wind grew still, my tears dried, and the turtle was nowhere to be seen. Only tiny bubbles rose from the bottom of the lake.

We stood in silence for a moment as the bay winds whipped around us. Then other friends shared prayers and a poem by Marie Rainer Rilke called "The Swan." Mary Ellen finished with a Tod Rungren song, which she modified for the service, titled "I Will Carry My Torch for You."

When the song was over, Jeff did a little more drumming. I took an envelope out of my pocket, containing some of Grandma's hair. I had collected it from her hairbrush before I left Illinois. I walked to the edge of the bay and let it go in the wind near the shore. Maybe the birds would use it for nesting material. A few strands remained in the envelope, and I wound them around my finger and tucked them into my hat before leaving the water's edge.

In Rockford the service continued with my sister Nancy sharing memories of Grandma. Her contribution was funny and sad and reminded all of us who Grandma was:

"Grandma made the most wonderful food, being from the South; she made our favorites when we came to visit. Country smoked ham and red-eye gravy, and lamb and mashed potatoes. She had a look that could

169

congeal blood. No one dare cross her.

"We all knew she had a special link with God. Every Fourth of July, on her birthday, she and Grandpa held their annual Fourth of July celebration. Every time it threatened to rain, Grandma told us that she had a talk with God that morning. She knew it would be clear for the party. It never rained on the Fourth, all the time we were growing up. . . .

"Each of her grandchildren was the most precious, most beautiful, most intelligent she had ever seen. Now I wonder, Who will stop the rain now that she's gone?"

Then my niece Laura read a poem, followed by a few words from Pastor Jim. He spoke about all the things she gave to us, her love of nature, how she fed several generations of foxes and birds out the back door of her home in North Carolina. He spoke about the meaning of the Lysne name. He concluded with stating the importance of releasing Grandma's spirit to light of God and gave a closing prayer.

Later that day I spoke to my family in Rockford. As we shared what occurred in the two services, it was nice to discover similarities and differences. A very precious part of the service in Rockford was by my red-headed nephew, who was only six at the time and wanted to remember Grandma and be included. All he knew from Cub Scouts was the Pledge of Allegiance. Since Grandma was born on the Fourth of July and very patriotic, his contribution fit right in. He stood up next to the flag in the chapel in full uniform and recited it to Grandma. He honored her memory with the best gift possible.

Creating Your Own Memorial Service

Perhaps you are mourning the loss of someone you love. Asking for help at this particular time is very important. If you are surrounded with loving community, this is a time to let them support you. If you feel isolated in your grief, there are many people who would be willing to help if only they knew of your situation.

There may be a local church that would be a comfortable place to request a service. There may be a favorite spot in nature that feels more comfortable. The first thing to figure out is where you want to hold the service. The second comes with dividing up the tasks. Perhaps you have a friend who is musical, or someone who would be willing to share a poem or story. A clergy person would help with the bulk of the arrangements.

Here is a checklist of some questions to ask yourself in preparation for creating a memorial service for someone you love:

1) Where do you want to hold the service?

2) How is the deceased represented? Will there be a burial or cremation, or will there be flowers, candles, and perhaps a photograph in their honor?

3) Who would you want to officiate or coordinate the service?

4) Is there someone who can handle the details, such as newspaper announcements, flowers, and memorial donations?

5) Who else wants or needs to be involved?

6) What songs, poems, and stories are there to share?

Here are two formats that roughly correspond to the services honoring my grandmother:

Rockford	California
Opening prayer	Forming the circle
Bible reading	Smudging or purifying with sage, cedar, or water
Statement of why we're gathered	Song
Sharing of family stories	Song
Poem	Sharing of story
Song	Prayer
Sermon, closing remarks	Poem
Closing prayer	Song, closing drum, prayers, release Grandma's hair

Of course there are other ways to structure your service for your particular needs. Don't forget the kids—they may have something important to share too.

34
Respecting Living Elders

Grateful Hands

You gave with open hands,
it was enough,
thank you, thank you.

Now, I place in your hands
my ring, this ribbon,
thank you, thank you,
I stand on your shoulders.

Joan and her parents had gone through a lot. They had supported her through her therapy, and attended many family counseling sessions together. Joan had stopped trying to change them and found a sense of peace. She could speak more honestly about her feelings than ever before. After all the years of pain, they were finally developing a friendship.

She wanted to honor her parents in some way while they were still alive. A party seemed inappropriate. Her expression needed to be deeper. She had read about tribal people who honored elders at certain times in their lives; perhaps she could create such a ritual in honor of her parents.

The day she arrived to visit them, Joan announced that she wanted to share something special. They were delighted and curious. The dining room table was the scene of so many games and projects, arguments and reconciliations, it seemed the perfect place to center the ritual.

Joan removed the tablecloth and pads to exposed the wood. She placed three different colored candles on one side. Then she placed the chairs in a semicircle, facing the candles, and seated herself between her parents. She removed from her purse two small gift-wrapped boxes. She felt nervous but confident.

"What's going on here, Joany?" her father blurted out.

"I have a something special I want to share with you," she replied. She reassured them that it wouldn't take long and it was important to her. "Is that all right?" Marge and George nodded in agreement.

Joan lit the candles and looked at each of her parents. "To me these candles symbolize the three of us. We are different but we have the same essential flame inside. Mom and Dad, I know it hasn't always been easy to be my parents. It hasn't always been easy to be your child. We don't always agree, but I know you did the best you could. I want you to know that it has meant a lot to me. I decided to celebrate the good things that are here between us. I want to give you each a little something that represents my gratitude and love."

She placed a small box in her dad's large, wrinkled hand. He looked at her sheepishly and opened it. A broad grin spread across his mouth. It was a swimming metal Joan had won in college. "But this is your favorite one, Joany."

"Dad, I wanted you to have it. You came to so many meets. I remember how you supported me, in so many other ways, too." She pined the ribbon on his sweater. The metal hung from his chest, glistening. They smiled at one another and she hugged him.

Joan pushed a small box over to her mother, who had tears in her eyes. "Oh, Joany, you didn't have to do this," she protested as she opened the box. Marge's eyes grew wide. She threw her head back and let out a hoot. "Joany, I love it!" Nestled in the box was a ring that Joan had received from her grandmother, Marge's mother, when she was a child. It wasn't fancy but had meant a lot to both of them. Forty years ago Marge had told Joan that she loved that ring and would take it if Joan didn't keep it safe.

Joan continued, "You have both given me so much. These gifts symbolized the love and caring I received from both of you. I wanted to say thank you."

Joan's father scooted his chair back and said, "Joany, we have something for you." From the hall closet he pulled out an old mahogany box. Returning to the table, he said, "Honey, I was going to leave this for you when I passed on, but I want to give it to you now." Inside the box were pictures of aunts, uncles, and grandparents. Each one was labeled with the name, date, and occasion of the picture. "These are your roots from both sides of the family. The box came from Grandpa Joe's cigars. I used to keep marbles in it when I was a young boy. I've kept it all these years."

For the rest of the evening, George and Marge told Joan stories about her family she'd never heard. They talked about their childhood, parents, sisters, and brothers. The candles burned low before they were finished. When it came time to part, Joan took their hands and said, "Thank you for this. I'm so glad you didn't wait to give me the pictures. I

173

wouldn't have known any of this." The three of them hugged. Then Joan blew out the candles.

Creating Your Own Ritual

Too often people wait to honor their parents at the funeral, instead of expressing love to them while they are still alive. Showing them your appreciation can be very healing and foster deep levels of communication.

Even though many people need to heal their past with their mother and father, there is an end to the process. Once one figures out what needs can and can't be meet by the family of origin, it is easier to let go of the expectation that they should meet all your needs. Then you are free to find ways to give to yourself what you missed.

It is helpful to the process of reconciliation to realize what you did receive as a child, and appreciate your family for what they gave you.

1. Begin by writing down the things you received as a child; start with a random number of, five, ten, or twenty things. This will help you flush out what you may have forgotten. What you learned from your parents could be as simple as tying one's shoe, or cooking, playing baseball, or receiving your first doll.

2. Next make a list of things you needed as a child that you didn't get. This is your childhood wish list. Today, as an adult, give yourself those things, or ask a friend to help you. This is important for closure, for clearing up any lingering resentment. You may want to give each thing to yourself in a ritual way, drawing a circle of love around you, and letting yourself cry.

3. Find something from your past, or make something that you value, and set aside a time to create a rite around it with your parents. Perhaps inviting them out to dinner, or giving it to them at Thanksgiving, can make it a unique and special celebration.

Appreciating your family is not always easy. Some people come from abusive families, and appreciating them is just not possible. Others are confronted with fears of rejection or abandonment, which are intensified because of the emotional wounds they may have received as children. It may feel to some as though they are putting their head in the tiger's mouth to express sincere feelings to their family.

Healing your fear can be a good reason for doing a rite. If you keep in mind that your intention is showing your appreciation and healing your fears, you can release the outcome and create an atmosphere of safety for yourself and your parents. Remember, if you approach your family with sincerity, there won't be room for them to make light of an authentic gesture.

SECTION FIVE

RITES WITH
THE NATURAL WORLD

35
Natural Disasters

In a Flash

It all comes from nowhere,
a gust of wind,
a few drops of rain,
the flaming match,
earth turning over in her sleep.

Ripping away
what we thought to be important,
what we knew was.
To feel the terror
of the disappearing home,
of friends and family
lost in a flash.

Maybe it's all to remind us
how small we are,
how precious
and expendable
at the same time.
Humbled to the power
of unleashed elements,
way too much of a good thing,

How much we take for granted, until,
ruthlessly,
we are shaken by what we cannot see.
How the two articulate,
the seen and the unseen,
like clouds floating through cutout trees
like blue sky around outstretched fingers
wide open
then suddenly,
      clasped together.

There was nothing they could do but run. The roar of the fire came down the Oakland hills so fast no one had time to do anything else. Marge and Alan had made their home on the Oakland hills for years, and, suddenly, one Sunday afternoon, everything was gone. No warning, just gone.

The firemen evacuated their street as the flames rushed down the slope. They could hear homes exploding above them. When they got to the bottom of the hill, everything was chaotic. Firemen blocked off roads; hundreds of people just like them were waiting at the bottom of the hill to hear of what was left. They found some neighbors who told them of people who were incinerated in their cars, the winds blowing the fire down the hill faster than they could move out of its way.

Now, days later, Marge looked over the rubble. She sat down on the front steps and cried. Alan sat down next to her and held her in his arms. He was crying, too. Everything they had worked for was ashes. The worst thing were the pictures—photo albums full of memories, her mother's antique bureau, the quilt her grandma made, Alan's golf clubs, their cars just burned out chassis.

"We'll rebuild, honey. We have insurance; we can rebuild," Alan said to reassure her.

"Some things will never be replaced—your father's paintings, Mom's bureau . . . Oh Alan, I can't think of starting over just yet," Marge said through her tears.

Then from the top of their driveway they could hear, "Oh, my God," as Marge's sister Bess and her husband, Don, came running toward them. "They said they were letting people back in; we came as soon as we could. I wish you had called us earlier—I had no idea."

"The phone melted along with everything else," Alan said somberly. Marge chuckled through her tears. "The phone melted! What a thought. Maybe it's still here somewhere."

The three of them stood together, Bess's arms around them both in a long embrace. Bess and Marge walked over the threshold of the house arm in arm. Alan and Don stood in the remains of the doorway. The fireplace was, ironically, the only thing remaining. The four of them poked around in the ashes and found the strangest things.

"Look at this; so far we have a fireplace poker, this box your mother gave us, the teapot, a few earrings and bits of jewelry, and this vase," Marge said with a sigh.

"There's more—I know there is," Don said optimistically.

"Not much more, Don, but it is—what is. My God, everything, poof!" Marge said, throwing her hands up.

Bess and Alan gathered the charred items and placed them on the front stoop. "Look at this bottle—it's melted into a puddle," Bess remarked. They all starred at the puddle of glass. Then the four of them gathered around what remained. Marge reached for Alan's hand, and then Bess and Don spontaneously completing the small circle, joining hands. They stood around the items for a minute in silence.

Then Marge said quietly, "Thank you for our lives, thank you for these few things that remain." She picked up a charred earring and put it on her ear. "I am so grateful for our friends and the love of our families. Please help us rebuild—help us let go of what was and rebuild." She reached down and touched the teapot. "May I be able to serve tea to my friends again real soon."

Then Alan spoke. "Help us to know what to do next; help us to learn what it is we need to learn from this. Give us the next steps with clarity and love. Let this box Mother gave us symbolize that life continues even in the face of loss." He placed the remaining jewelry in the box and closed it. "This melted bottle is now a paperweight, which I'll use at the office to remind me to live life today."

Bess looked up and through her tears saw streaks of tears running down the ash-covered faces of Alan and Marge. "Bless this land and the next steps for Marge and Alan," she said. "May this vase be full of flowers soon, as a symbol of finding joy in the ashes. Help them find peace."

Then Don said, "Please help all the people here who have lost their homes, their animals, and members of their families. Give them the help they need to start over."

Marge squeezed Alan's and Don's hands, the squeeze went around the circle, and they all dropped hands. Without saying a word, the four of them went back to poking around the ashes, and the long task of cleaning up.

Shaken to the Core

"Ah, this is where I need to be!" I thought as I touched my paintbrush to the paper. Just then the whole house began to shake; the concrete basement floor was undulating, cracks ran across where there hadn't been any before. Judith came running out of her apartment.

"I guess this is an earthquake?" I said, half joking, half scared out of my wits.

"Yes!" Judith screamed. "Get into the doorway, quickly!" She was hysterical.

"It's okay, Judith, we're okay." But the shaking just kept going. When it finally stopped, we were holding on to each other.

"My God, that was a big one!" Judith shrieked.

"Will there be more?" I asked.

"Yes," she said somberly. "This is just the beginning."

A few minutes later we heard on the radio what was happening around us. In the Marina district of San Francisco everything was on fire. A section of the Bay Bridge had fallen midspan. A freeway in downtown Oakland had collapsed. The entire city center of Santa Cruz had been destroyed. And new reports of damage continued to roll in. Over the next several months we experienced aftershocks—from a few seconds to rolling waves that felt like they went on forever.

A month after the quake I was sitting in my housemate's room, talking about the aftershocks, when a large one shook us so hard I nearl fell off the chair. I clenched my fists and sprang to my feet.

"That's it! I can't take it anymore. I'm going to Calistoga tomorrow!" I said, exasperated.

"What are you going to do up there?" Annie asked.

"I don't know, take a mud bath, I guess. I have to make peace with the earth again. My body is so tense I can't relax. I'll make it my ritual of reclaiming balance and trust. I have to do something."

The next day I drove to Calistoga, a town two and a half hours north of San Francisco, famous for its hot springs and mud baths. I found a suitable spa and checked in. In a few minutes I was lying in a rectangular vat of warm mud. A small Guatemalan woman was heaping mud all over my body. The smell of sulfur and other minerals surrounded me in the steaming goo.

"Don't move—you sink," the women said in broken English.

"Okay!"

As I lay there relaxing various parts of my body one at a time, I recalled all the destruction the earth had wreaked in the past month. The mud oozed around my toes and fingers as I wiggled them. The comfort of the mud felt so good to me. I felt nurtured and soothed for the first time in weeks.

As I looked at my mud-covered body, I suddenly saw my breasts and belly as the hills I had just driven through on my way to Calistoga. I saw the earth as a much larger, more voluptuous woman rolling over in her sleep. I moved my torso a little bit just to simulate her movement. The mud felt solid and liquid at the same time. I sank deeper into the vat, tensed a little, then relaxed, remembering the words of the Guatemalan woman. I was like the earth herself, who stretched and yawned her green and brown body.

I playfully drew a 'road' on my belly with my finger. I chuckled and something in me let go. I no longer felt a victim of the quake. It was as though I knew better what happened. I could flex with the great mother if she moved.

After a while, the woman came back and signaled me to lie still. She rolled a ball of mud in her hands, then started at my neck and rolled a fat layer of mud off of me. My pink chest and belly felt the cool air. She repeated this procedure on my arms and legs and around my neck and back when I sat up.

"The earth is healing," I said to her.

"Si! Mud good for you." She smiled and her eyes twinkled as she spoke. As she helped me stand up, I was flooded with gratitude for this wonderful woman who helped me heal. I imagined she knew a lot more about the earth than those of us raised in this country. I felt grateful to the earth for the support we take for granted every day.

As I showered I realized more deeply than ever before that the earth gives us everything we need—food, shelter, clothing, and medicines for healing—everything we need to survive and thrive. If the earth needed to move around a little, that was fine with me. After all, I was part of her, and she is in and all around me.

Creating Your Own Ritual

I hope you never experience a natural disaster in your lifetime. However, with our continually changing earth—its floods, fires, hurricanes, and quakes—it's likely that you or a relative will. The following rites are to help you help yourself grieve and move on if and when the time comes. It doesn't matter what the element—earth, wind, fire, or water—people often experience loss and gratitude at the same time.

Americans are finding some unique ways to grieve our losses such as the AIDS quilt which is several football fields long and still growing. We have taken an American folk art form and used it to celebrate the lives of the men and women who have died of AIDS. The Vietnam War Memorial has become America's wailing wall. It is helping to heal the wounds of that tragic war.

People need to come together after a tragedy, be it a death, a lost home, a natural disaster, or a war.

Recently, after the five-hundred-year flood of the Mississippi and

182

its tributaries, the town of Coralville, Iowa, had a "Flood Survival Party," where the town council sponsored a work party to take down the sandbags that had protected the town. It signaled the official end of the flood that year and helped the people move on.

My sister and her family were flooded on the Iowa River and used humor to relieve the long days of high water around their home. First they tied rubber ducks to the mailbox. Then they put in their basketball hoop a plastic blow-up doll with Edvard Munch's painting The Scream printed on it. Laughter truly is the best medicine.

Humor can also be incorporated into rituals. After my experience in Calistoga, humor was the factor that helped me let go. I felt a complete shift in my sense of safety after my visit to the mud baths. Friends who lived through the Oakland fire used it in creating small rites for themselves through the rebuilding process.

Outlined below are simple yet profound ways you can help yourself should you be in a natural disaster. Remember, different tragedies require different actions and rites; however, the following questions might help you create more healing:

* How can I reclaim balance with the elements?
* What will help me feel safer?
* What is my instinct telling me I need to do to heal?
* Whom do I want to join me?

36
Rites with the Earth

Rim of Fog

along mountain base
light on
willow strands
lilac bush
oak-
a million green coins

ducks are swimming
sun streaks my face
and warms it.

Why does nature
in its revelatory simplicity
matter?

Mountain is my bread
fly my humm
light
on leaves on
ducks swim
through this presence,

a calm of place
the river
this circle of
fog
lifting.

Why Create Rites with the Earth?

You might be asking yourself, why do a ritual for or with the
Earth? What will I get out it? Will I feel anything differently? How will it
make a difference for me or my family?

I can answer by saying that when I have done rites of the moon, honoring mensus, or rituals with others for the Earth, I always feel more connected and centered at the same time.

There is something else too. This is where we begin to dive off the rational into intuitive experience completely. When you create a rite for or with the Earth, you feel more connected to life by developing a relationship with the Earth herself. You feel more connected to yourself as a part of nature. The Earth will speak to you. Really.

Some of the rites with the Earth, can be as simple as a food offering at meals, sitting

in the woods alone, or creating rites around campfires when camping with friends. We need to establish a relationship with the Earth, so we then have the capacity to ask her for things we need on a spiritual basis, not only physical ones.

Rites can also be created in groups to ask the Earth what she needs from us for a change, instead of always taking from her without even a thought about it. Many people talk with the Earth, and they are not crazy. If we listen, she will tell us what she needs. But we need to start acknowledging that the Earth is not a commodity but a living being that we are in relationship with in any case. Do we want that relationship to be one of disregard and raping her, or of gratitude and awe? While this sounds simple, the best I can do is demonstrate it with a story to share my experience.

Offerings for the Earth

When I was involved in Native American traditions, one of the practices of many traditions is to do what is called a 'spirit plate' at meals. Every day, every meal, I offer a little food on plate to the spirits of the land and the animals. I have small plates or bowls that I use. Take a small amount of food and set it outside. Offer it to the Earth with thanks. Do it with the intention of saying thank you and developing a relationship with the Earth through prayer. You do this by asking to connect with her. Corn-meal, tobacco, grains, vegetables, or any food that you eat can go on the spirit plate. It makes a difference. I have done this for years, and it really helps me stay connected to the land and the spirits of place. All parts of the Earth have spirits that live around you on the land. These spirits appreciate that humans want to connect with them. Sometimes they show up when you offer them food. One of the easiest ways to become closer with the Earth is to offer her something that we have grown or cultivated and changed by cooking, drying or canning. The earth appreciates connecting through small food offerings, and she enjoys how we transform the food by cooking or canning it.Another practice is to offer the Earth some tobacco or cornmeal when you are out hiking or

biking. Before you walk, thank the Earth for her guidance and blessing and she will watch over you and take care of you. You can also ask your Angels. It works. It helps to stay centered. It helps to become more connected and protected.

Rituals for the Moon are discussed in Section Two, Rites for Humankind, and more specifically in Chapters Thirteen, Fourteen and Nineteen. Including men isn't difficult, just include them as it is appropriate, and focus on the Moon as reflection of our lives. The moon each month are named already, (See: https://www.nationalgeographic.com/science/space/solar-system/full-moon/) and you can follow Solstice, Equinox and monthly moon celebrations that are individual, and not complicated, by simply setting your intention for the full moon, and new moon each month. You can also support this in a group, with a simple ritual.

The full moon helps us affirm our life intentions for work or home life as they are, and the new moon can give us a new start every month with new things we want to bring into manifestation. The Earth and solar system gives us everything we need to thrive and live with fullness and renewal.

Feeling Our Relationship to the Earth

A group of us were heading up to the gold mine country of Mt. Umunhum at the southern end of the San Francisco Bay Area, south and west of San Jose, California. We were with a group of people interested in celebrating the Earth.

Daniel Foor, Ph.D. was the leader, and I was along because I needed to be. After several years of living in Santa Cruz and being in married life with a husband and family, I found myself single again and living on my own. My husband had moved to Puerto Rico, his homeland, my step-children were grown and I was trying to gain my bearings in my new life alone.

I had never heard of Mt. Umunhum, which means Hummingbird. In fact I had never been on top of any of the mountains in the San Francisco Bay in all the twenty-three years I have lived here, except for Mt. Tamalpais. That fact alone compelled me to discover more about the mountains and the earth that we are surrounded by in this beautiful place.

Now I am not an ordinary traveler in rituals. I had experienced many Earth-based rites through dancing with various Native American tribal groups on their reservations to studying the Umbanda tradition in Brazil over the previous twenty-five years or so. All of the ceremonies that I had attended had been supportive for my understanding and my comfort with this new group of ritual workers.

Though we barely knew each other I trusted Daniel as we had met a few times learning about each other's work and talking about the Earth. He was about half my age, and I was quite impressed with how much he had accomplished as a young person in his early 30's. He was about to get his Ph.D. in psychology, and he was already practicing with an M.F.T. license. He had abandoned a traditional practice for an Earth-centered one.

As one of the older members in the group, and somewhat out of shape, I was enjoying our excursion, but getting rather tired. I had never seen the Bay from this vantage point. It was so beautiful to see all of the other mountains surrounding the San Francisco Bay, from Mt. Hamilton, to Mt. Diablo, to the Sonoma Mountains to Mt. Tamalpais. All of them were visible from this trail we were walking up and down. The bay itself was visible as a bright blue hazy jewel. Daniel had a particular idea of where we were going and what we were to do up there. He had scoped it out and knew right where to take us.

Before we reached this spot we stopped at some Bay Laurel trees. Daniel had us find a tree that was willing to offer us some leaves for a ritual for the Earth. He offered tobacco to the "right" tree. He intuited which tree was the right one. We could have offered our hair, or corn meal to the Earth before we took a leaf or branch. We listened for the 'answer' from the tree whether it would be willing to do so. The tree complied by a feeling of 'yes.' Except for the use of Bay Laurel, all this asking the plants for permission was consistent with what I had learned in my ceremonial work with the Lakota and Annishnabe tribes. 26 Bay Laurel was something we used instead of sage or cedar, which we would burn, because of the fire danger in California. It made sense. The Bay Laurel was abundant medicine everywhere around us.

After brushing each other off with the green pungent Bay Laurel branches, we then began to sit in a circle outside where a waterfall was running by the trail. Daniel led us to a very secluded spot off the trail where all eight of us could fit next to this waterfall among rocks, ferns and Bay Laurel trees.

You could not see the creek from the trail, as it was covered entirely with low branches. Under the trees there was an enchanted fairyland of mist and water gently falling over the rocks. I found a spot that seemed comfortable and put my back to a rock face and wedged myself between the wall and a huge boulder so I could rest my back. All of us found our spots in a rough circle.

We called in the four directions, honoring the elements, the Earth, Sky and Center. We could feel the four directions close to us as we closed our eyes and listened through our hearts. Then Daniel asked us to go inside in silence and ask the mountain what the mountain needed from us.

That was something quite new to me. I had never done this before. In all my years of Earth-based ritual practice with tribal groups, I had never asked the Earth what it needed from me. Usually I was asking for help.

As Daniel rang a bell that he brought with him, I went into a meditative state and I felt serene. Then I asked Grandfather mountain the question; "What do you need from us?" As soon as I asked the question, I felt as though I was a volcano and the Earth was speaking through me. It was not gentle, I felt the Earth wailing and I began to sob uncontrollably. Tears streamed down my face, and I could not contain my crying. I felt physical pain that was not mine. It came up through me as the Earth's pain.

As we walked to this spot on the mountain, Daniel had schooled us, in the history of the Mt. Umunhum area. For many years, it had been dotted with mercury mines in the Almaden area and the Guadalupe River on the other side of the mountain was terribly contaminated with mercury. The waters of San Jose contained higher than normal levels of mercury as most of San Jose drew water from the river. The mines, though discontinued now, were full of deep tunnels that went all through the mountain. While many of the other mountains in the Bay Area had become nature preserves, this mountain had been the sight of indentured labor with Mexican, Native American, Welsh and Chinese with hundreds of people dying in the mines between the 1850's until the 1940's when the mines were closed. That is when the military had moved in and claimed the top of Mt. Umunhum as a look out post for Japanese aircraft. They had built many buildings on top including a cement tower that marred the contour of the mountain. Lead paint created toxic environment and rats lived up there carrying a deadly bacterium that made the place unsafe for humans to go up to the top at all. It was sealed off entirely.

What I was experiencing was extremely uncomfortable. As I tried to gain my composure after he sounded the bell for us to 'come back' from our conversation with the mountain, I found myself feeling as though I was fried from the inside out emotionally.

188

Daniel helped me back to the group and asked if I was all right, though I could hardly respond. Everyone had his or her own experience of the place. Some were enjoyable experiences of the water, flowers, ferns, bay laurel trees and rocks. We each shared our experiences over lunch.

But I couldn't eat or talk. At the end, he gently turned to me, and asked what had gone on and if I wanted to share it. As I did, relaying the pain of the place, others listened and some had felt the same thing with less intensity. Due to my recent losses of my marriage and of my family I must have been more open. But after I shared, Daniel told us more of the terrible pollution that existed to that day on the top of the mountain. I had tapped into something that was real. The mountain had pain that humans created and it was expressing it through me.

Subsequent trips to Mt. Umunhum had resulted in others feeling the pain of the place more intensely and me feeling less pain and more joy than the first trip. Eventually, I brought my own group to the area of the closed mines, and we did an honoring ritual for the Earth by laying flowers and tobacco in a wheel and praying for her health and welfare. Some of the group could also feel the pain of the place, though each time it was less and less as we went to experience the mountain.

What I learned from these excursions was how much the Earth hurt, just like us, and that we can help her. I also learned that all of the ways that the Earth hurt were the same ways that women or men felt when violated by others who disregarded, raped or harmed them physically or emotionally. It came from the same negative attitude of disrespect and taking what one wanted without permission.

In the Lakota Sioux language there is a word; "Wasechu," which for the longest time I thought meant, "white person" in a derogatory way. But over the years, as I hung around various dances and participated in them, I learned it meant "those who take." Lakota and other Native Americans saw the attitude of the white settlers as one where they take what is not theirs without permission. The clash of cultures was also a clash in consciousness. The Lakota and all indigenous tribes lived sustainably with a relationship to the Earth that was reverent and integrated with her. The settlers who came to this country came with the idea that the land was free for the taking and that the Earth was theirs for the exploiting of it. Also there is a Western attitude that the Earth is something to be concurred and dominated rather than to work with in relationship.

Now, as a group, we were returning to the Earth as white, brown, black and mixed race people honoring her, and recognizing the pain we humans have caused. Every visit was a little less painful, and we felt blessed and welcomed to help. She asked us to help clean up the Guadalupe River on several occasions and Daniel and many of us wrote letters to help encourage Federal legislation to Senators and Congress to encourage help with the cleanup of the top of the Mountain.

After that request that came from the Mt. Umunhum, we did several river cleanups, engaging schools and young people and wrote letters to support the clean up. Senator Mike Honda implemented federal stimulus money to address a superfund site to clean up the top of the mountain and to fix the problems that the military and the mine owners left behind. The Ohlone people were instrumental in making the Mid-Peninsula Regional Open Space on the mountain into an educational place for visitors and to once again hold sacred ceremonies, as the mountain continues to be a sacred place for everyone. I like to think we had something to do with making Mt. Umunhum a happier place for future generations.

Doing Your Own Ritual with the Earth

While not everyone will have this experience of the Earth's pain, you can begin to listen to what she needs in your area. One book I found helpful was Living with the Spirits of the Land, A Spiritual Memoir, by Barbara Thomas. In it she recalls how she became connected to the spirits of the Earth and how she talks to them to support the consciousness that the Earth needs at this time, and that we need too. Her guide Mano has told her: That the Earth can no longer go it alone, and neither can humans." We need each other; Earth, Humans, Cosmos.

Here are some ideas. Gather some friends. Ask the four directions to help you, call them in, with Earth, Sky and Center, and listen to her, then ask the questions in the silence of your own meditation; What do you need, Mother Earth? How can I help? When you are done, don't forget to open the four directions back up and release them, or you will have more intensity than you bargain for in subsequent days.

Each season can be honored as well, through recognizing the Solstices and Equinoxes. These seasonal times of Spring, Summer, Fall and Winter, change us as we move through them. They can help us experience our own inner changes and what is needed for the area that you live in now. Simply taking a moment to acknowledge these transitional moments help us enjoy the Earth in a more connected way.

The phases of the moon can be a powerful way to experience the our own phases, especially for women. I outline several ways to honor the moon phases in Chapters Thirteen, Fourteen and Eighteen.

The following are samples of Rites for the Earth you can do with friends. This way various land configurations can be acknowledged and honored depending on where you live.

Honor the Waters, Beach and River Clean up with Rites of Passage

Mother Ocean in many Earth-based traditions is called the Yemanja, Iemanja, Mother Ocean, and the "Great Cemetery." She takes things, and never returns them, like the dead, or those things that we no longer need. She also cleanses us, if we let her. Here are some ways to help the Ocean and that the Ocean can help us.

Acknowledgment is very powerful. Buy or cut some white roses, then offer her the roses and thank her for what she offers you. You could combine this ceremony with a beach cleanup. I pick up trash on the beach as I walk it, whenever I walk the beach.

Fresh water is the source of life that we must have to survive. Honoring and talking to her can be an amazing experience. Take some yellow flowers, or a small amount of tobacco, and breathe into center yourself, offer it to the river or a nearby creek in deep gratitude. Listen. She will speak to you. You can combine this with a river cleanup. Thank her for being a part of your life.

In a recent meeting with a spring at Panther Meadows on Mt. Shasta, I was guided to create a ceremony for myself. When I was there, I first called in the four directions, Earth, Sky and Center, I offered a small pinch of tobacco, and asked the spring to share information about a future relationship. I felt I was beginning a new phase of my life. The spirit of the spring replied, and we sat together as sisters, while she spoke to me about the man I would be with soon. She gave a description, and told me the time frame when he would be available and want a relationship that was healthy and grounded. Then she showed me what he looked like, and I was increasingly curious. I closed the ceremony asking that it be in alignment with my highest self and my teachers, after which I opened the four directions and gave thanks.

Honoring the Air we Breathe-This might be best done in conjunction with any other ceremony, on a mountainside, or in a place where the winds are more common. Some places, like Mohave and Tehachapi Mountains have constant winds in certain spots. Use incense or some sage to honor the air. Thank it, for giving you life. Listen to the wind; it may have something to tell you about change. However, never do this ceremony if it will set off sparks to start a fire.

Honoring Fire as Teacher-In the Huichol tradition, Grandfather fire speaks to you through the fire once you make an offering of a stick, tobacco, chocolate, or corn meal. While this is not a traditional Huichol ceremony, it does borrow from that tradition. This is a great way to deepen your relationship with the fire, and help you connect more deeply with friends.

Gather a group of friends, and begin with the four directions around a campfire. Have ready sticks from the surrounding trees, small sticks, four to six inches long. You can also offer small squares of chocolate or coco beans, tobacco or cornmeal. Use these offerings to listen to the Fire. Pray for what you need, or ask for help. Grandfather fire always gives you an answer.

37
Fire Circle

Using the Four Elements
to Support Monthly Community Rites

Gabe and Ira were gathering wood for the fire. It was a warm summer day, and it had been dry and hot. However they knew it would cool down at night, so the fire would feel good. After going through some red tape with the landlord who happened to be Gabe's boss at the coffee shop where Gabe worked they got permission to create a nice fire pit there. They had dug a pit in the backyard of the house they were sharing and laid stones they found from a field outside of town. Gabe knew enough to ask the stones if they would like to join this fire circle and protect the people.

As more people trickled in they pitched in and gathered as much wood as they could, around their small house that sat on the edge of town. This was Gabe and Ira's first fire circle. Both the young men had attended fire circles over the course of a few years. They had learned from a man who studied in the Huichol tradition. Their fire circle would be a little different. They had heard about how to manage one from their teacher and Gabe's teacher had been encouraged him to take on a monthly fire circle with his friends.

The purpose of this fire was to bring friends together, to support his friends in a deeper kind of community, and to give people that he cared about, a place to pray.

Ira had not had as much experience but had attended a few Huichol rituals. He liked the idea of finding a way to unite his friends in a circle without drinking or drugs. He despaired about how different everyone's experience had been growing up—some of his friends were Catholic, some, like himself were Jewish, and others had no religious base at all. So he wanted to see how he could bring everyone together in one place in a common way that might help everybody. It seemed to him that prayer was something all religions did, and with the passing of their friend, Lydia, they decided it was a good time. Lydia's death was the catalyst but it wasn't the only reason for them to gather.

Most of the people coming to this event had known Lydia, a smart vibrant girl who liked to use drugs. She had been sober for a few months when her addiction took over one night and she overdosed. There was a lot of loss, as other friends were still using too much and there were some that others were worried about. Most of his friends didn't know how to talk about this sudden death, as it was the first for a lot of people in his community.

Jennie and Melanie came with food, and others had bread and salads and a chicken. There were about ten of their friends gathered. When the fire was laid and they had eaten, everyone gathered in chairs and on logs around the fire pit.

Gabe started. "We are here to honor Lydia. Most of you knew her. We are also here to gather to find a way to pray. Some of us are out of work, some are having a hard time with parents or siblings, and some have had other losses. It seems that this fire circle is a way to pray and come together to find a way through our lives."

At that Gabe took a match and lit the fire and called in the four directions, saying: Spirits of the West, the place of the waters, of grief, of letting go, of release, please be with us, Spirits of the North, the place of standing alone, of being in our power, please be with us, Spirits of the East, of new beginnings, of starting over, please come and be with us, Spirits of the South, of family, of tribe, of birth and death please be with us. Great spirit who watches us, please be with us, Grandmother Spirit of the Earth come and be with us, and Spirit of this fire, come and be here to help us speak from the center, from our hearts."

Then as Ira tended the fire, Gabe passed a bowl of tobacco for each person to take some in their hand. When everyone had some tobacco, Gabe spoke.

"I am asking the Great Spirit for help for us to release Lydia to you. Please take care of her. And help us find a way to move on. Many of us knew her, and loved her. She was a good person who had a problem. I am asking for your help, because I loved her, and I know others here did too."

At that he threw tobacco into the fire, and then he took another pinch.

"Please, I need to find more work, I would like to work with other people, could you help me find the way through here, Should I go back to school or find more work? I am asking for clarity."

He threw the tobacco into the fire. The small cut leaves curled and turned bright orange. There was a slight scent of tobacco in the burning.

who gave instrumental feedback and support during the last two years of

Then Jennie took her tobacco. She held it to her chest, and then held it up to the sky and tossed it in, not saying a word. Her best friend Anna was sitting next to her. Anna took her tobacco and asked,

"Please whoever you are over there that is watching us, could you help me? I really need to find work. I would like a job in a place that is cheery, where I could move around; I can't sit for too long. Kids would be fun, but I have to pay rent and I don't know if I can this month. Please help me find something soon."

The sparks from her tobacco seemed to help spark something in her.and they came back to Gabe, he asked if they wouldn't mind if he sang a song. He had a great voice. So he sang a song that he liked a lot from his teacher. It was an old Indian song. The words were more sounds than they were words. Then he sang "Blowing in the wind" an old Arlo Guthrie song his dad used to sing. This prompted some of the others to sing songs from their history. Ira sang a song from his Jewish faith, and there was laughter and peace that settled around the group.

Finally, as the fire died, Gabe released the four direction by saying: Spirits of the Center, the Earth, the Sky, of the South, East, North, West, thank you for coming and please take our prayers to the four directions, hear our prayers.

Everyone sat there together, and no one wanted to leave. So they sat together around the fire, finding other songs they all knew to sing.

Fire circles are great ways to come together with friends. I have been in various circles where people of all ages gather. I have also been in circles with just women where they gather every month to support each other with their moontime.

In one situation in my hometown, women gathered together every month during the full moon at different people's houses. They prayed for their children, for those who died, for those who w

As each of the young people tossed their prayers into the fire, ere struggling, they prayed for themselves. Every month they came back together to report the small miracles that had happened. It was a great relief, and a way to bond the community to help the whole group. In this case, there were no Indian songs, only one's about the moon, or circling. Sometimes they sang, and sometimes they didn't. But the prayers always helped.

If you live in the city, you can have fire circles in an out door fire dish, or pit, or if in an apartment, have a small bowl or pan that you designate for your fire ritual. You can also use alcohol in a metal dish for a low flame with cotton balls. Instead of tobacco, you can use prayers written on papers and toss them into the bowl one by one.

However you create this, you will find a way to bring people together. It is best if someone leads, gathering attendees through email, and someone else does the leading of the ritual. Then pass around the leadership, as this creates stronger community and gives everyone a chance to shine in their own way.

Conclusion

Most all of these rituals shared in this book are from true stories. A few are composites of people and places. What is most important is that each of us take up these important tools to empower us to create meaningful circles and soul level communications together for the good of all. This will heal relationships, move us forward in evolution, and help us become more present with one another, no matter our politics, or sense of place.

In regards to the Earth and our relationship to her, we need to see that the Earth is a living being, and she is also the greatest healer there is, so that we can recognize the importance of Divine Mother, in the Earth, in the Stars, and within ourselves. We need to begin to honor the feminine in ourselves, male, female or mixed gender. She knows how to heal herself, as well as provide healing herbs and medicines for us. Recognizing her balances male domination we seem to have to over come at this time in our human story. Love heals all things and we are bombarded with love every day from the Earth and the Sky, if we allow ourselves to feel it.

The Earth will, however, in the coming years, need our help as the Earth warms from our pollution. We need to listen to her, and we need to begin to see how her advice, through all our scientific brilliance, will be simple, effective and straightforward. So let's listen to her more deeply, and see how we can accept her advice, and then follow it. All of this will help us be more present with ourselves, our place on the planet, and our individual relationship with our common Mother.

About the Author

Robin (White Turtle Woman) Heerens Lysne has always been interested in cultural diversity and creativity. The main question that drove this book was; "How does one bring to white people the depth of Native American culture without appropriating their culture?" Another one was; "How does one inspire people to think about their lives in order to bring more meaning to daily life?" A third was; "How does one goes about creating culture towards transformation?"

Born and raised in the Midwest, her writing reflects the lanscapes of her first home in Rockford, Illinois, later in Michigan, and her love of California where she has resided since 1987. She has been a Sundancer, and Ogitchidaah Equae, or woman of the Ogitchdaah, an Annishnabe (Ojibway) dance where she received her spiritual name, White Turtle Woman. Today she is a devotee of Divine Mother, and Yogananda.

She earned her M.F.A. in poetry from Mills College in 2012. In addition to her writing, Lysne is an artist who has shown widely from NYC to Santa Cruz, CA. Her artwork explores cultural and spiritual themes embedded in nature.

She is the author of six previous books, the last one *Mosaic, New and Selected Poems*, published in 2017, *Poems for the Lost Deer*, published in 2014, both by Blue Bone Books, Santa Cruz, CA. Other books are: *Heart Path Handbook, Heart Path Learning to love Yourself and Listening to Your Guides*, also by Blue Bone Books, Santa Cruz, CA, and *Living a Sacred Life*, and *Dancing Up the Moon*, published by Conari Press, Berkeley, CA.

Her interest in personal transformation extends into her work as a professional medium, psychic and Energy Medicine Practitioner. In her 30 years experience she offers her clients safety, intuitive insight and compassion. In 2013 she earned her doctorate in Energy Medicine from The University of Natural Medicine, Santa Fe, NM. She offers trainings, and workshops on energy medicine, shamanism and rituals, giving others support in their personal transformations.

The creator of Blue Bone Books, which she started in 2006, includes a collective poetry press with five other poets from her Emerald Street Poetry critique group, a group that has contiued for over 20 years.

Today she lives and works in Santa Cruz, CA. Her websites are: www.thecenterforthesoul.com and www.bluebonebooks.com.

Acknowledgements

Many people contributed to this book. Some I will name here and others, because of the personal nature of the book, will not be named. Most names within the rites have beenchanged to respect individual privacy. The exception is when talking of my own experiences, or those of people who have given me permission.

In this new 2018 edition of *Ceremonies from the Heart*, I would like to thank Daniel Foor, Ph.D. author of *Ancestral Medicine* for providing us with a ritual for the Earth to listen to her pain human's have caused.

Thank you to the elders of the Huichol tradition who have generously shared their traditions with us. Also thank you to Craig and Christine Balletta, and Raven Barto for supporting me with rites that they shared with me, and I with them. Thank you too to Suzy Ross, Ph.D. who has shared her work on transformation, and who I had many late night text and phone conversations with on Rites of Passage. She is the author of the forth coming book on transformation called the *Map to Wholeness: Finding Yourself through Crisis, Change and Reinvention* (North Atlantic, 2019). Special thanks to the Mother Earth, and my dear friend Barbara Thomas for her inspiration and shared interests and her book, Living with the Spirits of the Land, A Spiritual Memoir (Thomas, 2018).

The original volume, called *Dancing Up the Moon*, would not be in your hands without my agent Kathy Altman, Right Hand Productions, Mill Valley, CA. Kathy responded to my manuscript with enthusiasm and heart. Mary Jane Ryan, editor and publisher of Conari Press in 1995, has my deepest gratitude for recognizing the intention and possibility of the original Dancing Up the Moon and for her clarity and editorial assistance. For all of the fine staff at Conari Press, I wish to express my thanks for their careful handling and creative input.

Important editorial advice came also from Barbara Brauer of Wordsworth, Margaret Albanese, and most especially from Anna P. Lewis, who patiently edited many segments of the manuscript, as well as provided vital feedback with her razor sharp clarity and honesty. Her creative writing companionship and inspiration provided a light at the end of the tunnel during many lonely days of writing.

Special thanks to Clive Matson and the members of the his Thursday class, Sharon Davies, Robin Cayton, Sharon McDonald and others writing. Their companionship has been a touchstone of quality and clarity for me.

Additional encouragement came from my dear friends and colleagues at Commonweal. During my stays as a massage therapist for the Commonweal Cancer Help Program (CCHP), in the 1990's I wrote much of this manuscript. Michael Learner, Ph.D., provided contacts, an office space and encouraging friendship and sound advice, the late Vivakan Flint, Nadine Parker, Jon DeKadt, Jnani Chapman, Christine and Jim Boyd, and Jenepher Stowell, in their unique ways, assisted and supported me. I would like to especially thank Marion Weber, mentor and artistic friend, Waz Thomas, outrageous fellow poet in arms, and Rachel Naomi Remen, M.D., mentor and friend who contributed generously to the chapter on Rituals of Lament, the surgery and breast cancer segments. Her advice and support are greatly appreciated.

I am deeply grateful to the Flow Fund, New York, for its grant support at a critical juncture in the writing of Dancing Up the Moon and The Marina Counseling Center for providing the non-profit container for the grant. Bob O'Brien, Ron Moshontz,

Laurie Agee and the board of directors have my heart felt appreciation for their support and faith in me. Thanks also to Ann Hubble Maiden for bringing me to the Marina and sharing her work with me on children.

Additional encouragement came from Charles Terry, Vice President of International Center for Integrative Studies, Candice Fuhrman, Michael Toms, JoAnn McAllister and Steven Toth. Riane Eisler, David Whyte and the late Angeles Arrien, Ph.D. have inspired me through their work, integrity and encouraging words. The late Maria Gimbutas is remembered for her courage and inspiration. Through her work, that of Riane Eisler, Starhawk and Luisa Tiesch, I have been inspired to create rites that resonate with women and men today.

Many, many thanks to Jennifer York, Pen, Marleen DeNardo, Lincoln Howell, Barbara Bissell Howell and Alisha for their willingness to share their stories. Their living examples will encourage anyone who reads them. I am deeply grateful to the late Joy Bol for putting me in contact with her daughter Jennifer.

My parents, the late Robert and Martha Heerens, have supported this book with reading and feedback and encouraging words since its inception in early 1980's. I am truly grateful for their openness of mind and heart. Their faith in me helped sustain me. My sisters and brothers-in-law, the late Kisti and very much alive Sid Beckwith, Jill and David Windahl,

Nancy and Ralph Heerens-Knudson, Sara Heerens, all have helped in their personal ways. My nieces and nephews, Lysne, Ben, Nathan, Tobin, Erin, Laura, Nicolas, Keegan and Tyler, were the original inspiration for the adolescent rites. I hope they see the Blue Heron Ceremony as a beginning family chronicle. I am grateful to everyone for being willing to venture into an experiment that became a family tradition. My grandparents, Walther and Jo Lysne, and Karen and Joe Heerens and the rest of the Heerens/Lysne, Nash clan gave me roots, a sense of humor, respect for tradition, a family of which I am proud and wings. Grandma and Grandpa Lysne participated in the first ritual for Lysne and Grandma the second with Ben, providing her love and support with the grace of a heron. Special thanks to my cousin Michele Pambrum Witt, who shared her thesis on Apache puberty rites for girls, and the ceremonies that she did with her children, which are in this book.

My friends who have been there with exceptional support and inspiration, are storyteller Mary Ellen Hill, Robyn Michelle Jones, Amita, Janet Trenchard, Jeff, Therese, Margaret and Bretta Grumley, Paul Bibbo. Most of them as well as Ruth Kissane, Helena Young and Jim Gilkey, Vern and Julie Rogers, Marsha and Noah Bartholomay, Blake and Veronica Basham, the late Elizabeth Daughert, Kim Farmer, Ellen Flowers, Phil Branch, Elaine and Art Riechert, Margaret and Dallas McClemons, Dana and Ethan Jain, Barbara Phillips, and Norine Nicholson are friends who I have done ceremony with for many years and who have been spiritual friends and supporters. Thanks to Marsha Bartholomay for providing the women with a moon lodge and our monthly ceremony in the heart of Oakland, CA.

Thank you Elsie Carr for providing me with a safe and beautiful place to write, as well as a lovely home and easy friendship in the last months of writing.

The members of Jackson Area Dance Council, Monette Thorez, Julie Guy, Nancy Lodice, Sally Pesetsky, Paulette Burgess, Kathyrn Green, Diane O'Brien, Lisa Cole and Toni Miller provided me with the first opportunity to perform `Feather and Claw'. I am very grateful to dancers Nancy Lodice, Monette Thorez and Julie Guy for their interpretation of `bird and cat'. Thank you to the late Lisa Cole who sewed and co-created the perfect costumes for the performance. Thanks to my friends and the staff of the Ella Sharp Museum, Jackson, Michigan, the late Mildred Hadwin, the late Lisa Cole, and Lynnea Loftis. I am deeply grateful for their encouragement and support during my tenure. My earliest research for rites of passage for children were done for the Arts Go To School Program at the Museum. Thanks also to Ted Ramsay and Coco for inspiring me to go for it.

Dancing Up the Moon began as my thesis on adolescent rites of passage, which was completed at The Institute in Culture and Creation Spirituality (ICCS), Oakland, Ca. My deepest gratitude goes to Matthew Fox for creating ICCS and Brian Swimme both of whom provided such a rich environment in which to grow. Also to the Sisters of Holy Names College, where the Institute was housed, provide a beautiful setting in which to learn.

While at ICCS, I received special editorial help and mentorship from Daniel O'Leary, Madeline O'Calleghan, Marleen DeNardo, James Conlon, Matthew Fox, Brian Swimme, Bob Frager, Paula Koepke, Robert Rice and Jeremy Taylor who were all instrumental in the early development of *Dancing Up the Moon*.

Special thanks to instructors Starhawk, Luisa Tiesh, and Buck Ghosthorse, who gave me so much food for the soul and put me through the rites from their cultures. Their work has deepened my connection to Spirit and forever changed me.

In addition I would like to thank the Friends of Creation Spirituality, Matt Fox and Susan Espinosa for the grant I received in 1988, which sprang from my work with adolescents.

Others who helped in my research and provided places to experiment are Sharon Thomas, in her gifted classroom in the Charles City Middle School, Charles City, Iowa, and Ron Hunt, Minister at Community Congregational Church, Tiburon, CA.

Thanks also to ministers Carol Saysette and Frank Evans for being so receptive to my work. Special thanks to the children in both those places for receiving the material so well and providing valuable feedback to me.

My respect for and understanding of ritual tradition began when attending Kemper Hall in Kenoska, Wisconsin in 1970 and '71. My dear friend who I met at Kemper, Mary Ann Godfrey, introduced me to the Lakota sweat lodge ceremony in 1973, for which I am deeply grateful. Her tradition inspired me to begin my quest for rituals that work in the culture at large.

Although I will not write about Lakota Tradition out of respect to my teachers, I have internalized what I know of the Lakota teachings. What I have learned shows me everyday what Western culture has forgotten. The teachings help me reclaim my own ancestry and deepen my connection to Spirit. For their inspiration, prayers and profound teaching

I also would like to thank Lessert, the late Barrett Eagle Bear, Florentine, Larry, Richard, Grandma Mary, Karen and Ben, the Chubbs Family, Norman and all other leaders of the Four Winds Sun Dance, the Yucichupi Sundance and the Ghosthorse Sundance a big thank you for continuing your ceremonies and keeping them in-line with the Creator. To dancers and soul friends, Jeff and Therese Grumley and Fred and Karen Gustafson, I offer my deepest blessing and thanks for your courage and the opportunity to serve you and the path to dance in Sun Dance. Your prayers have helped me and this book.

And last but not at all least, to you the reader I give my thanks for receiving *Ceremonies from the Heart* into your hearts.

Honoring all my relations,

Robin White Turtle (Heerens) Lysne, Ph.D., August 30, 2018.

RESOURCES

Below are vision quest resources for people of all ages, and rites of passage groups. The inclusion here does not necessarily mean an endorsement, however most of these groups have been around for many years. Also if you do an internet search for your area, there will be many resources that will pop up.

All Kinds of Therapy
https://www.allkindsoftherapy.com

Animus Valley Institute-Bill Plotkin, Ph.D.
https://animas.org/

Eco-Psyche-Artistry Brian Stafford, M.D., Psy.D.
https://eco-psyche-artistry.com

Headwaters Out Door School
https://www.hwos.com/

Rites of Passage Vision Quest
https://www.ritesofpassagevisionquest.org/

Rites of Passage Journeys
www.riteofpassagejourneys.org

Rites of Passage Wilderness Therapy
https://ritesofpassagewildernesstherapy.com/

Wilderness is Medicine
https://wildernessismedicine.org/

The School of Lost Boarders
http://www.schooloflostborders.org

Vision Quest Wilderness Passage
http://www.brianwinklerphd.com/VisionQuestWildernessPassage.aspx
http://www.lifepassage.com/programs_vision4.html

Rites of Passage Wilderness Programs
http://www.rehabs.com

SOURCES

Arrien, Angeles, Ph.D. Signs of Life: The Five Universal Shapes and How to Use Them. Sonoma, Calif.: Arcus Publishing, 1992.

. The Four Fold Way: Walking the Path of the Warrior, Teacher, Healer, and Visionary. San Francisco: Harper San Francisco, 1992.

Art of the Dogon. Film. MuseFilmTV, Karl Katz Producer 1992

Barks, Colman. Like This. Translation of Rumi, MayPop Publishing ISBN 0-9618916-2-9, page 15.

Beck, Renee, Metrick Beck, and Sydney Barbara. The Art of Ritual. Berkeley: Celestial Arts, 1990.

Brown, Joseph Epes, ed. Bury My Heart at Wounded Knee, An Indian History of the American West, Holt, Reinhart & Winston,1970

Bly, Robert. Translation of Rainer Maria Rilke s poetry (n.p., n.d.).

BusinessBecause, on-line article, 3 Business Schools Leading The Way In Ethics Training. written by Caity Shaffer, Feb, 19, 2018

Byrd, Randolph C., M.D. Positive Therapeutic Effects of Intercessory Prayer in a Coronary Care Unit Population. Southern Journal of Medicine, vol. 81, no. 7 (1988): 26 29.

Campbell, Joseph. Hero with a Thousand Faces. Princeton: Princeton University Press, 1949.

Campbell, Joseph. The Power of Myth, with Bill Moyers. Doubleday, New York, 1988.

Campbell, Joseph, Mythos I: The Shaping of Our Mythic Tradition, a lecture series that Joseph Campbell gave at the end of his life. Joseph Campbell Archives.

Edwards, Betty. Drawing on the Right Side of the Brain. Los Angeles: Tarche, 1979.

Eggan, Fred, ed. Social Anthropology in North American Tribes. Chicago: University of Chicago Press, 1937.

Eisler, Riane. The Chalice and the Blade: Our History, Our Future. New York: Harper and Row, 1987.

Eliade, Mircea, ed. The Encyclopedia of Religion, vol. 12. New York: MacMillan, 1987.

Essene, Virginia. Secret Truths for Teens and Twenties, Santa Clara, Calif.: S.E.E. Publishing, 1986.

Fox, Matthew. Breakthrough: Meister Eckhart s Creation Spirituality in New Translation. Santa Fe: Bear and Co., 1980.

_. Original Blessing. Sante Fe: Bear and Co., 1983.

_. Reinventing Work. HarperSan Francisco, CA, 1993.

Ghost Horse, Buck. Red Nations Sacred Way. Oakland, Calif.: Privately published, 1986.

Gibbs, Jeanne. Tribes. Santa Rosa, Calif.: Center Source Publications, 1987.

Grualnik, David B. Webster s New World Dictionary. New York: Warner Books, 1983.

Higgler, Sister M. Inez. Chippewa Child Life and Its Cultural Background. Washington, D.C.: Government Printing Office, 1951.

The Holy Bible. London: Burns & Oates, 1954.

Houston, Jean. The Possible Human. Los Angeles: J. P. Tarcher, 1982.

Jung, Carl G. The Archetypes and the Collective Unconscious. Princeton: Princeton University Press, 1969.

_ The Symbolic Life: Miscellaneous Writings, vol. 18 of the Collected Works. Princeton: Princeton University Press, 1950.

Katz, S., and M. Mazer. Understanding the Rape Victim: A Synthesis of Research Findings. Hobokon, NJ, John Wiley and Sons, 1979.

King, Serge. Kahuna Healing. Wheaton, Ill.: Theosophical Publishing House, 1983.

Kingma, Daphne Rose. Weddings from the Heart. Emeryville, Calif.: Conari Press, 1993.

Lanckton, Alice Keidan. The Bar Mitzvah s Mothers Manual. New York: Hippocrene Books, 1986.

Lysne, Robin Heart Path, Learning to Love Yourself and Listening to Your Guides, and Heart Path Handbook, For Therapists and Healers, both by Blue Bone Books, Santa Cruz, CA.

Madhi, Louise, Steven Foster Caraus, and Merideth Little. Betwixt and Between: Patterns of Masculine Initiation. La Salle, Ill.: Open Court Publications, 1987.

Miller, Alice. Drama of the Gifted Child, The Search for the True Self. New York: Basic Books, Inc., 1981.

Mitchell, Steven, trans. The Selected Works of Rainer Marie Rilke. New York: Random House, 1982.

Gretchen Morgansen, Josua Rosner, Reckless Endangerment, Times Books, Henry Holt Editions, 2011.

Moore, Tom. Rituals for the Imagination. Dallas, Tex.: Pegasus Foundation, 1983.

Murdock, Maureen. Spinning Inward: Using Guided Imagery with Children. Culver City, Calif.: Peace Press, 1982.

Nelson, Gertrude Mueller. To Dance with God: Family Rituals and Community Celebrations. Mahwah, N.J.: Paulist Press, 1986.

Nishnobe, the Story of the Three Tribes, Menomenee, WI, Tribal Productions. 1984.

Paladin, Lynda S. Ceremonies for Change. Walpole, N.H.: Stillpoint Publishing International, 1991.

Pearson, Carol. The Hero Within: Six Archetypes We Live By. San Francisco: Harper and Row, 1986.

Perera, Brinton Sylvia. Descent to the Goddess: A Way of Initiation for Women. Toronto: Inner City Books, 1981.

Reese, Lyn, et al. I m On My Way Running: Women Speak of Coming of Age. New York: Harper and Row, 1980.

Susan L. Ross, The Making of Everyday Heroes: Women s Experiences with Transformation and Integration, Journal of Humanistic Psychology, 2017, page 16

Sex and the Spirit Article, Creation Magazine, vol. 3, no. 2, May/June 1987.

Sonoma County Rape Crisis Center. Booklet, page 2, 1991.

Starhawk. The Spiral Dance. New York: Harper and Row, 1979.

. Truth or Dare: Encounters with Power, Authority, and Mystery. San Francisco: Harper and Row, 1987.

Sullander, R. Scott. Grief and Growth: A Pastoral Resource for Emotional and Spiritual Growth. Mahwah, N.J.: Paulist Press, 1985.

Swimme, Brian. The Universe Is a Green Dragon: A Cosmic Creation Story. Sante Fe: Bear and Co., 1984.

Thomas, Barbara, Living with the Spirits of the Land, complied by Mary Jane DiPero, ISBN 9781720663546, published by Barbara Thomas, barbarathomas.info

Underhill, Ruth M. Red Man s America. Chicago: University of Chicago Press, 1953.

Van Gennep, Arnold. The Rites of Passage. Trans. by Monika B. Vizedom and Gabrielle L. Coffee. Chicago: University of Chicago Press, 1909, 1960.

Walker, Barbara G. Women s Rituals a Sourcebook. San Francisco: Harper and Row, 1990.

Webster s New World Dictionary of the American Language, Warner Books, Simon and Schuster, NY 2010.

Jennifer Wolf, about.com single parents, website

Woodman, Marion. The Pregnant Virgin: The Process of Psychological Transformation. Toronto: Inner City Books, 1985.

ENDNOTES

1   Mythos I: The Shaping of Our Mythic Tradition, a lecture series that Joseph Campbell gave at the end of his life. Joseph Campbell Archives.

2   Joseph Campbell, Hero with a Thousand Faces, page xxiii.

3   Robin Lysne, Heart Path, Learning to Love Yourself and Listening to Your Guides, and Heart Path Handbook, For Therapists and Healers, both by Blue Bone Books, Santa Cruz, CA.

4   Webster s New World Dictionary of the American Language, Warner Books, Simon and Schuster, NY 2010.

5   The Chinese would say there are five, the fifth being metal. However, metal is part of the earth, and I include it there. I choose to reflect the traditions of the Americas, where there are four elements, because it is the land we live on in the United States. My personal experience of nature is more keenly reflected in the four elements rather than five. Your tradition may not support my theory, and I honor what you choose to express.

6   Besides Native American naming ceremonies where the dreams of the parents matter in forming the names of the children, some African cultures name children in a similar way. Meledoma Somé discusses this naming ceremony in his books, Of Water and Spirit, Ritual: Power, Healing and Community. Eastern cultures such as Japan have ceremonies several days after birth and do not traditionally name children for elders as is commonly done in western societies.

7   Joseph Campbell, The Power of Myth with Bill Moyers, page 82.

8   Joseph Campbell, The Power of Myth, with Bill Moyers, page 83.

9   Susan L. Ross, The Making of Everyday Heroes: Women s Experiences with Transformation and Integration, Journal of Humanistic Psychology, 2017, page 16

10   Ibid. page 16, 17.

11   Ibid. page 18.

12   Website: Jennifer Wolf, about.com single parents

13   Reckless Endangerment, Gretchen Morgansen

14   BusinessBecause, on-line article, 3 Business Schools Leading The Way In Ethics Training. written by Caity Shaffer, Feb, 19, 2018

15   The Rite of Passage," Van Gennep, Arnold, University of Chicago Press, 1960, p.85.

16   from the PBS series with Bill Moyers, The Power of Myth .

17   Van Gennep, Arnold, The Rites of Passage", 1909, translated by

Monika B. Video and Gabrielle L. Coffee, 1960, The University of Chicago Press, Chicago, Illinois

18   Ibid.

19   Van Gennep The Rites of Passage" , pg. vii, introduction by Solon T. Kimball.

20   Jennifer Wolf, About parenting.com : Here are some statistics that show us where we are today. Of the 84% of custodial mothers: 45% are currently divorced or separated, 34.2% have never been married, 19% are married (In most cases, these numbers represent women who have remarried.) 1.7% were widowed. Employment statistics are even more shocking. 79.5% of custodial single mothers are gainfully employed; 49.8% work full time, year round and 29.7% work part-time or part-year, while of the 18% fathers who are custodial parents: 57.8% are divorced or separated; 20.9% have never married; 20% are currently married (In most cases, these numbers represent men who have remarried.) Fewer than 1% were widowed. 90% of custodial single fathers are gainfully employed and 71.7% work full time, year round and 18.4% work part-time or part-year.

21   For girls doing vision quest, it is very important to have them out in the wilderness when they are NOT bleeding. This is true generally when they are camping as well, especially in areas where wild animals can smell the blood, like bears, mountain lions or wolves.

22   Sappho, fragment 34, Lobel-Page 34, Cox 4, loose translation by Tom R. Burch

23   These statistics are from the 1979 study, Understanding the Rape Victim: A Synthesis of Research Findings, by S. Katz and M. Mazer.

24   This information is from the Sonoma County Rape Crisis Center, 1991.

25   Kingma, Daphne Rose. Weddings from the Heart. Emeryville, Calif.: Conari Press, 1993.

26   26 Bay Laurel is a very strong medicine for clearing sinuses and the head. Because of fire danger in the Bay Area, and throughout California, we were being extra careful. Bay Laurel is not present in the Midwest nor East Coast. There, we would have used sage, and we would have lighted the dried sage or cedar to smudge or smoke ourselves off. Ceremonially, this is done before any ritual.

Made in the USA
Columbia, SC
12 October 2018